THE HIGH SCHOOL DOCTOR

The *Underground* Roadmap to 6, 7, and 8 Year Accelerated/Combined Medical Programs (BA/MD) in the United States

NAGENDRA SAI KONERU, M.D.
VINEET ARORA, M.D.
OMAR WANG, ATC

© 2002 by Nagendra Sai Koneru, M.D., Vineet Arora, M.D., Omar Wang, ATC.
All rights reserved.

No part of this book may be reproduced, stored in a retrieval system, or transmitted by any means, electronic, mechanical, photocopying, recording, or otherwise, without written permission from the author.

ISBN: 0-75966-621-0

This book is printed on acid free paper.

FOR MY WIFE SARITA AND OUR RESPECTIVE PARENTS……

ACKNOWLEDGMENTS

We would like to thank our respective families and friends who have given us much support throughout our endeavor. We would like to thank all of the medical students and fellow physicians who responded and gave us invaluable input regarding their medical school experience. Special acknowledgements to Sunita Koneru for helping us with the legal issues of the book, and Ashish Khanna for writing the chapters on the resume, standardized tests, and personal statement. Finally, we would like to acknowledge all of the medical schools and the AAMC for providing us with information about each of the specific accelerated medical programs.

Sincerely,

Nagendra Sai Koneru, M.D.   Chicago, IL
Vineet Arora, M.D.   Chicago, IL
Omar Wang, A.T.C.   Macon, GA

CONTENTS

FORWARD IX

PREFACE XI

LET'S PLAY Q&A 1

CHOOSING A COLLEGE 5

SHOW ME THE MONEY 11

MEDICAL SCHOOL AFTER HIGH SCHOOL? THE ACCELERATED MEDICAL PROGRAMS (BA/MD) 15

THE STANDARDIZED TESTS 20

THE *UNDERGROUND* TIMETABLE FOR HIGH SCHOOL STUDENTS 26

THE UNDERGROUND HIGH SCHOOL VIGNETTES 30

THE UNDERGROUND RÉSUMÉ 32

LETTERS OF RECOMMENDATION 35

THE PERSONAL STATEMENT 37

THE INTERVIEW AND THE THANK YOU LETTER 40

THE AFTERMATH 45

THE CRÈME OF THE CROP: THE BEST UNDERGRADUATE AND MEDICAL SCHOOL PROGRAMS 46

ACCELERATED MEDICAL PROGRAM LISTINGS 51

THE ACCELERATED MEDICAL PROGRAM PROFILES 59

THE BEST ACCELERATED MEDICAL PROGRAMS 114

THE FUTURE OF MEDICINE 116

FORWARD

The Journey by Vineet Arora, M.D.

In starting this endeavor almost 5 years ago, it is worth mention that by the time you are reading this completed work, I have gone from medical student to resident to chief resident to fellow and am now embarking on my career in academic medicine. There are several concrete underground tricks that I have learned in this journey, the most useful of which has been communicated on preceding chapters. However, it is not these concrete tricks that inspired this creation. Looking back at my journey, it is the milestones of becoming a doctor that I remember most. Some milestones are evident, marked by an end or a specific day. However, even more intense are the subtle milestones you cross and don't even realize it. To understand this special underground journey, I urge you to join me in reviewing some of the major milestones.

Medical school and residency is more than just the development of a career and professional skills, but it is the making of a *doctor*. Medical schools recognize this transformation and most have indoctrinated a first day white coat ceremony/Hippocratic oath to acknowledge humanism in medicine. Nearly two years later, after you take regurgitate everything you have learned in 40 hours of class during step I of the boards, you will wear this white coat when you are taking care of your first patient in the ward. They might even look at you with hope and call you doctor. You turnaround, and wonder who they are talking to. You are there to learn. The next milestone perhaps is the day you graduate medical school. Congratulations, you now have an MD. But are you a *doctor*? In the eyes of your friends, family, credit cards, and student loan financers, you are. Think whatever you want for this brief juncture prior to the start of your internship a few short weeks away. The truth is on the other end of the phone during your first call night. A nurse calls you and says "Dr., the new patient on the floor is complaining of _____ in this area, and he is in a lot of pain. He doesn't look so good." With a trembling unsure voice, you will say "Uhh, I will call you right back." Universally, you will not know the answer to half of the questions you are asked. However, you will learn from your mentors and from countless hours of direct experiences of firsthand patient care. For the next few years, you will become sleep deprived, question your medical knowledge, look at friends who have money and time, and wonder if you did the right thing. This is normal! Not only will you sacrifice, you will suffer, but don't give up, you will heal…Then, sometime during the middle of whatever residency you do, radiology, dermatology, internal medicine or surgery, you will cross a point where maybe you made the right call on the CT, EKG, or did the appendectomy by yourself. Rejoice, you are now a doctor, *technically*. But are you a *doctor*? At an unpredictable moment, there will be a turning point. It is not only confidence in skill, but importantly the behavior and belief that you are acting for the good of your patients. In striking instances, it is a single experience with an emotionally charged but difficult ICU experience or a distraught family member that moves you to rise above the ordinary. In other cases, the summation of experiences, both positive and negative, that will define your clinical skills, ethical and professional beliefs, and your empathy, all of which make you the *doctor*.

Truthfully, medicine is a sacrifice of great proportions. Furthermore, the reward is intangible, delayed, and as illustrated by milestones, easily overlooked. It is the intangible and delayed rewards that sometimes lead to inner turmoil along the journey. It should be no surprise that during this long and arduous process, many individual's frustrations exceed the inner satisfaction derived from being a *doctor*. They may switch careers, or more alarmingly, work full time but in professional and personal despair. Your best weapon against a life of professional despair is to not only know yourself, but explore yourself. Similar to choosing a college, be armed with the information to make good decisions. Furthermore, do not make decisions that place yourself in environments that you will not be happy in. Sounds simple, right? Keep this in mind when you are choosing your career in medicine. For instance, it doesn't matter how interesting you think surgery is, the question is can you survive the long hours?? If yes, that's great. But if you know that is incompatible with your future life and a good outlook, don't even think twice about it.

You cannot be a good doctor if you cannot be a good person. This translates to your personal and professional relationships in your sphere. Of course, it is natural for your relationship with others, physicians, friends, family and patients to be under tremendous stress during the training process. The key to success is an instrumental support system that will reenergize your low battery. For some, this is support is living close to family. For others, organizations such as religious groups or sport clubs provide this support. Last but not least, discover the hidden, but enourmously powerful crutch built within you. Your internal stress management systems will serve you well. This may come in the form of any outside interests, travel experiences, reading, or even thinking. I urge you to identify your support systems, use them effectively, and most importantly, take care of them. Eat regularly, sleep, exercise, make your doctor and dentist appointments. Try to stick with your hobbies, call your friends and family often. Once you have effectively maintained your support systems and can use them when you are in need, you will be amazed with your life, personally and professionally.

PREFACE

Choosing a career is one of the most important decisions you can make in your lifetime. Unfortunately, the medical career has become such a competitive career choice that many students don't even consider it an option. Vineet and I both realize how difficult the application process can be for both students and parents. In high school, we don't often think about our career choices. Our career seems so far away. However, when you are considering medicine as a career choice, it is never too early to think about what you can do to make yourself a good candidate for medical school. If you are a college student reading this book, you will have already come to realize the challenges that lie ahead of you. The rigorous course load that you will have taken in your undergraduate years is only the first step in becoming a physician.

This book has taken 5 years to come to fruition. It was a simple idea that Vineet thought of during her second year in medical school. Bobby also joined the project when he entered medical school. Because of time constraints and the content of the book, five years was justified. We hope this book about accelerated medical programs and will give you a great insight in determining what type of college is right for you. We also hope that you will know exactly what these accelerated/guaranteed medical programs are looking for in a candidate. Finally, we believe that the uniqueness of this book will give you a competitive edge when applying to the medical school of your choice. We wish you the best of luck!

The authors welcome any type of comments from the readers. If you find any errors or additions that you feel that we should take into consideration in our next addition, then please let us know and we will place you in our contributors list.

Please note that all entries will become property of the authors and will become subject to reviewing and editing. Please send all submissions to

nagendrasai@hotmail.com

varora2000@pol.net

omar_wang@hotmail.com

THE HIGH SCHOOL DOCTOR
The Underground Roadmap to 6, 7, and 8 Year
Accelerated/Combined Medical Programs (BA/MD) in the United States

Let's Play Q&A

> *He who asks is a fool for five minutes, but he who does not ask remains a fool forever.*
> *-Old Chinese saying*

So, you are a high school student or college student and you are considering medicine as a possible career choice, huh? Are you crazy?! Maybe you are. In any case, you probably have loads of questions! Well, you may have just found all of the answers in this book.

But before we dive into the main content of the book, lets play a game. The question and answer game.

You can be the questioner and we, the authors, will answer them. We have compiled some very important questions that we think will be informative for you. Any questions that we did not answer for you can be directed to us personally at our respective emails and will answer them for you personally. Ok, Let's play...!

Is it too early for me to start thinking about medical school?

No. Because of the competitiveness of medical schools today, it is never too early to plan your life around being an ideal candidate for medical school. Competitiveness aside, medicine and medical school is an extremely large commitment.

You will be in school for at least another 8 years, with a few exceptions that we will discuss soon. After medical school, you will be in training as a medical resident for at least another 3-7 years depending on the specialty of medicine you may choose. Thus, medicine is a field that should be given much thought before entering. You definitely don't want to be one of those individuals that goes through 8 years of schooling only to decide that medicine is *not* for you.

However, we stress that you can only read about the medical field to a limited scope. The true weight of your decision should rely on experience.

How do I get into medical school?

Applying to medical school is much like applying to college at the undergraduate level. Medical schools have certain requirements just like most undergraduate colleges.

NAGENDRA SAI KONERU, M.D.
VINEET ARORA, M.D.
OMAR WANG, ATC

Every student applying to medical schools within the United States has to take the Medical College Admissions Test (MCAT). In addition, there are several course requirements that must be fulfilled for acceptance into medical school from the undergraduate level. Due to the competitive nature of medical schools, you must be able to maintain an exceptional grade point average, participate in extracurricular activities, and have some letters of recommendations that make you look like a star.

Just to put into perspective, there are medical schools that receive up to 160 applications per seat! In other words, for one spot of acceptance, you would be competing against 160 other well qualified individuals.

What is the MCAT?

The Medical College Admission Test (MCAT) is a multiple choice, standardized examination created to assist admission committees of medical schools to predict which of their applicants will perform adequately in the medical school curriculum.

The test measures problem solving, critical thinking, and writing skills in addition to the examinee's knowledge of science concepts and several prerequisite subjects that are relative to the study of medicine. The MCAT is scored in each of the following areas:
Verbal Reasoning, Physical Sciences, Writing Sample, and Biological Sciences. U.S. medical schools require applicants to submit MCAT scores before applying for admission.

Is there anyway the process of getting into medical school can be made easier?

Yes. Back in the days where your parents were smoking pot and PCP, medical school application rates were much lower than they are today. To promote well qualified high school students towards medicine, several medical schools started programs entitled "BA/MD" programs.

There are several other names which you may be familiar with such as "combined medical programs", guaranteed medical programs, or "accelerated medical programs." These programs offer conditional acceptance into medical school right out of high school! These programs can range anywhere from 6-8 years. For example, the 6 year programs would require you to do only 2 years of undergraduate school and then accept you into medical school which is always 4 years.

Several of these programs will take applications up to the sophomore year in undergrad! Today, there are over 50 BA/MD programs throughout the United States.

What about foreign medical schools?

Foreign medical schools have been known to be less competitive than U.S. medical schools. In fact, many of our peers in residency and medical school rotations have come from foreign medical schools. From our experience, some of these foreign medical schools train students very well and some don't. Ultimately, if you decide to go to a foreign medical school, you must realize that responsibility relies heavily on you.

Also remember that you if you want to come back into the United States, there are several tests that you must pass such as the USMLE step 1 and 2 (United States Medical Licensing

Examination). Statistics show that foreign medical students have a significantly lower pass rate on these examinations than U.S. medical students. Does this mean that foreign medical schools are not as good as U.S. medical schools? Not necessarily.

One fact that should be considered is that most foreign medical schools use different testing formats than what is used in the United States. For example, medical schools in India test all exams with pure essay questions, while the USMLE tests are all multiple choice.

Can I get into a foreign medical school right out of high school?

The answer is yes! However, this does not apply to all foreign medical schools. Some foreign medical schools require you to take the MCAT. In a scenario where an MCAT score is needed, it would be wise to finish as much of your undergraduate requirements as possible to have enough preparation for the exam.

There are many foreign medical schools that do not need any entrance examinations. These schools normally take students right out of high school. Check out our book on foreign medical schools entitled *The Best Foreign Medical Schools: The Underground Roadmap from Foreign Medical School to United States Residency*.

Do I have a chance of getting into an accelerated medical program?

We aren't going to lie. These programs are highly competitive. There are several requirements to get into these programs. You need to have a minimum SAT score or ACT score just to be considered for many of these programs, most of which are above 1300 on your SATs and above 30 on your ACTs. However, we feel that this book will give you have an advantage over other students. It is also important to remember that every program may not be for your liking. *This book will help you get into the right program for you.*

So how do I do well on the SAT or ACT? At least well enough to get into one of these ridiculously competitive programs?

We will give you several tips in this book which will give you a plan for studying for these exams. We have also included an appendix at the end of the book with a list of several study resources that will make your studying more efficient.

Will I be less prepared at an accelerated medical program?

From our own experience and from talking to other students who have gone through other programs, the answer is no. The bottom line is that you cannot slip through medical schools in the United States without being qualified. There are the USMLE (United States Licensing Examination) steps 1 and 2 which every medical student must pass to graduate. These tests are not easy, and from our analysis, students from BA/MD programs have a pass rate equivalent to the national mean.

NAGENDRA SAI KONERU, M.D.
VINEET ARORA, M.D.
OMAR WANG, ATC

All this schooling business sounds pretty expensive. I don't know if my parents can afford to support me through medical school. What do I do now?

We have included a chapter on financial aid that will answer all of your questions about affording BA/MD programs or any university that you decide to attend.

Assuming I achieve the minimum requirements, how do I know which one would suite me best?

Keep reading. We have outlined all of the important considerations that you should make when thinking about BA/MD programs. After you have realized what is important, you can look at our detailed profiles of each of the BA/MD programs to make the ideal selection for you.

Do you have any more advice?

This book is not an advertisement or promotion device to convince you to go into a BA/MD program. This book is simply here to inform you of the different programs and possibilities. The High School Doctor was also written with the intention to make you the most ideal candidate possible for any choice that you may make. Good luck on your journey my friend.

Chapter 2

Choosing a College

*Two roads diverged in a wood, and I—
I took the one less traveled by,
And that has made all the difference.
Robert Frost, The Road Not Taken*

From the looks of things, it is not easy to get into a medical school, but you probably already knew that. One thing that sets you apart is that you are already ahead of the game. Most people decide that they want to go to medical school sometime during their college career. After this, these students start to research the various options and routes to enter medical school. However, by that time, a lot of critical decisions affecting their status as an applicant to medical school have already been determined.

For instance, it is too late to go back and do more research or take that semester abroad when you are already applying. In fact, the most crucial of these decisions affecting your chances of getting into medical school is made three years before you start the application process for medical school — the choice of the undergraduate college. There are many sources that will tell you that it does not matter what college you attend or major you choose because you can still take the pre-medical requirements and enter medical school.

However, one of the things that is most misleading about that statement is that depending on your choice for college and major, you will need to focus on different areas of your application to strengthen your status as an applicant. In choosing your college and major, you are automatically dictating your advantages and disadvantages in applying to medical school.

Depending on what you choose, it is of utmost importance to maximize the advantages and minimize the disadvantages that your college carries with it in order to improve your overall success. It is worthy to note that there is no universally correct choice for college. Everyone is unique and has different needs.

Depending on your personality and preferences, you may be more prepared to deal with the disadvantages of one type of option than another. In order to assist you in your decision, we will outline the four major options for college and the advantages and disadvantages each option carries with it.

NAGENDRA SAI KONERU, M.D.
VINEET ARORA, M.D.
OMAR WANG, ATC

The four major options for the high school student who wishes to attend medical school are the following:

(1) The state university
(2) The private college heavily associated with a reputable medical school (large percentage of pre-meds)
(3) The private liberal arts college with or without a medical school (small percentage of pre-meds)
(4) The university/college with an accelerated medical program (also called BA/MD or early assurance)

The State University

The state university is traditionally one school that everyone automatically applies to whether it be as a "safety school" or the school of top choice. Because so many high school students have the state university as one of their options, it is especially important to consider the pros and cons of attending the state university overall and in terms of medical school acceptance. We will start with the general pros and cons of attending the state university.

General Pros:

Let's face it — not everyone's parents have bank accounts the size of Warren Buffett's. The state school is by far the cheapest option out of the four routes listed above. With state-subsidized tuition, four years could cost you and your family less than one year at a private college. Many pre-medical students opt for their state school for undergrad education solely for this reason. In addition, a few pennies saved here will definitely help with the rising cost of medical education that you will have to face four years from now.

One particular scenario of not is that bright high school students in some states are offered cash incentives and scholarships in order to attend the state school. When deciding between this officer, and an acceptance at a big name private school, it will be important to consider how much the tuition breaks/scholarships will be worth to you and your family.

There is something to be said about a familiar environment. This is especially important for students who can see themselves being very homesick away at college. A depressed pre-med cannot be a successful one. No, this does not mean live at home for the rest of your life. But living in a dorm close to home does have its advantages. You are close enough to go home or to meet up with old friends whenever you want to get away, and you will soon learn the value of having mothers do laundry and cook delicious meals! It also keeps transportation costs down — maybe you can convince your parents that by going to the state school, they are saving so much money on airfare, you should be able to take vacation trips to your favorite hot spots.

In the general scheme of things, the social atmosphere at a state school will be more relaxed than at a private school. In other words, there will always be slackers and people who are taking seven years to graduate. The Greek life and social opportunities are also more numerous. Most importantly, you are at school with about 10,000+ people. Someone will always be throwing a party or be ready to go out.

Because of the immense size of the state institution and state-subsidies granted to the university, they are able to offer an extremely diverse variety of curricula, programs, majors, and services. For example, many state schools have everything from the hard-core sciences (math, physics, engineering, biology) to a full range of the humanities/arts (philosophy, sociology, dance, music, etc.).

It is important to remember that this is one of the major advantages your school will have since most private schools don't have the infrastructure to support such a diverse curriculum. You should definitely fill your schedule with classes that interest you in all sorts of fields with this kind of course offering.

General Cons:

Most of the disadvantages to this institution lie in the immense size of the state school. Because there are so many people, it is very hard to shake the "just another number feeling" that many students often reject the state schools for. Many of your core classes in your major will be very large classes. It will be very difficult to know everyone, or be able to do everything that you want at a school with this size.

A limiting factor of the state school is in the student body makeup itself. You are essentially going away to college with students that come mostly from your own state. While this still represents a diverse body of students and opinions, it will never provide the same sort of insight and exposure as attending a private school with students from all over the country and other parts of the world.

You are not attending one of the prestigious elite Ivy League colleges; if you choose this route and if you are bright student, this can be a little deflating to an ego. You will be in a situation of proving how smart you are to others because the college name will not be able to do it for you.

Medical School Standpoint Pros:

Because there will definitely be pre-meds at this school, there will definitely be a pre-med advising system. This point needs to be researched further from school to school because some state schools have better success rates for medical school applicants than others.

Because of the wide variety of curricula and programs, it is very easy to distinguish yourself as an interesting candidate. This is a point that needs to

be capitalized on fully. If you attend a state school, you cannot overlook the fact that your school offers an interesting array of classes and extracurricular activities. Medical schools look for distinguishing features in every candidate and the opportunities to distinguish yourself at a state school are far more numerous.

Statistically speaking, there are some state medical colleges who prefer students who are graduated from the state university. A more extreme case of this are state schools that offer an early admission program to medical school during the sophomore or junior year that bypass the normal application process. These schools will be further discussed in the BA/MD section.

NAGENDRA SAI KONERU, M.D.
VINEET ARORA, M.D.
OMAR WANG, ATC

Medical School Standpoint Cons:

One of the largest disadvantages to attending the state school is the large number of pre-meds at the school. This means large pre-med classes with lots of competition in those classes because only the top students will be able to gain admission successfully.

Among the medical school admissions deans and population at large, there is a general perception that state schools are easier than private schools. Whether this is true or not of course varies on an individual school basis. In any case, it is rumored that there are admissions officers at top colleges who do say that a high GPA from Harvard is more impressive than that same GPA from a state school. More often than not, however, a 4.0 from any college will speak for itself.

Of notable exception to the above pros and cons are the state schools which have honors colleges/programs that admit top students from that state. These honors programs attempt to recreate the atmosphere of a more selective college by only admitting talented students and offering special classes and curricula for these students.

Admittance into this program would generally alleviate the disadvantage that the general perception among medical schools is that state universities are easier. In addition, opportunities such as research and teaching assistantships are more plentiful for these honors students than the general student body.

The Pre-Med Factory

The pre-med factory is the term for the private college that is associated with a reputable medical school. In other words, because of the reputable medical school associated with the undergraduate college, many medical school hopefuls like yourself attend such institutions under the myth that they are at an advantage as a pre-med in getting into medical school. The typical example of a school in this category would be Johns Hopkins University or Washington University in St. Louis which have well reputable medical schools associated with the university. However, before being blinded by the name and prestige associated with these schools, it is very important that you open your eyes to some of the disadvantages with the pre-med factory. We can start with the general pros and cons of attending such a school.

General Pros:

These schools, for the most part, are private and are more selective than the state university. Because of this, they are considered more prestigious and traditionally their name carries a great deal of significance.

Because these schools do not restrict their student population to primarily state residents, there is a diverse makeup of ethnicities, localities, and interests presented in the student body. The opportunity to meet students from all parts of the globe and from all sorts of cultures is a very enticing advantage to attend such a school. You will find this

to be one of the most enriching things about the college as this diversity is represented in all sorts of things from the student organizations to the social scene and dormitory life at the college.

Because these colleges are generally smaller than the state university, it is much easier to take a more active role in student government, social fraternities and sororities, and especially in athletic programs.

General Cons:

Because these schools are private institutions, they are not heavily subsidized by the state and this difference in subsidies is handed down to you as higher tuition. In most cases, the tuition of these private schools is more than double of your state university.

The social life, in general, is not as exciting as attending a state university. Most students are graduate school oriented, thus leaving an air of open competition. This creates an "uptight" feeling among many students, different from the more laid back state school atmosphere.

There will be lots of pre-meds at your college. This translates into large pre-medical classes which are required. As many as 300 students can be in your lecture. With the traditional mean-based scoring on the tests, it is very difficult to maintain high grades since you are competing against all bright students with the same intentions as yourself.

Medical School Standpoint Pros:

These schools will have a very strong pre-medical advising system because of the large percentage of pre-meds. Because a reputable medical school is associated with the undergrad, it is much easier to find a research opportunity at the medical school which will further enhance your changes of getting into the medical school of your choice.

These undergraduate schools traditionally have strong science programs which make for a strong pre-medical curriculum. You will have the chance to work with big name researchers and professors, whose recommendations can hold a lot of weight in your medical school application and interview.

Medical School Standpoint Cons:

Many medical schools will limit the number of people they can take from a certain region and school. This obviously makes sense since medical schools will strive to create a diverse entering class to produce a diverse array of doctors. However, the implications of attending a school with so many pre-meds means that the burden of distinguishing yourself from people at your college falls heavily on you because your choice of college is not a distinguishing factor.

Most likely, all of the competitive pre-meds at your college will have received good grades, good MCAT scores, done their share of research and participated in extracurricular activities. This means that there is one way to distinguish yourself — life experience. A semester abroad, an overwhelming business/political experience, extraordinary talents in athletics, music and arts are what admissions committees would like to see to make the decision between you and your lab partner.

The Private Liberal Arts College

You will find that these colleges are the hidden gems among paths to choose in going into medicine. Because they are private colleges, they share the same overall advantages in attending a private school. However, because these colleges are not pre-medical factories, it gives you the chance to explore your own identity a little further than the pre-medical persona.

General Pros:
These schools, for the most part, are private and are more selective than the state university. Because of this, they are considered more prestigious and traditionally their name carries a great deal of significance. There is usually a diverse makeup of ethnicities, localities, and interests represented in the student body. You will find the diversity as one of the most enriching experiences of this type of college.

Because these colleges are generally smaller than the state university, it is much easier to take a more active role in student government, social fraternities/sororities, and athletic programs. One advantage over the pre-med factory is the students are generally more laid back due to the wider variety of interests available to the students.

General Cons:
Because these schools are private institutions, they are not heavily subsidized by the state and this difference in subsidies is handed down to you as higher tuition. In most cases, the tuition of these private schools is more than double of your state university.

Medical School Standpoint Pros:
In contrast with the pre-med factory, this type of college has smaller pre-medical courses and fewer pre-meds. Generally speaking, the classes are less competitive and it may be easier to get better grades. The uniqueness of your school will be an asset in applying to medical schools. This is in general a reverse of the fact that pre-med factory students are a disadvantage because so many people from their school are applying to medical school. It is likely that you may be one of very many people applying to medical school from your college and this will look very interesting on your application. Medical schools want well-rounded doctors, so because you are at a liberal arts college, the chances to further distinguish yourself and add to your life can be taken advantage of.

Medical School Standpoint Cons:
Because there are fewer pre-meds at this college, the pre-med advising system is less likely to be very efficient. What this means is that in order for you to apply to medical school, you will have to do more research on your own and be more aware of deadlines than someone at a pre-med factory. Because there is no hospital or medical school attached to your undergraduate college, the opportunities to do research or make connections with medical school faculty do not exist and you must seek these opportunities elsewhere.

THE HIGH SCHOOL DOCTOR
The Underground Roadmap to 6, 7, and 8 Year
Accelerated/Combined Medical Programs (BA/MD) in the United States

Show Me The Money

> "To give away money is an easy matter ... and in any man's power. But to decide to whom to give it, and how large and when, for what purpose and how, is neither in every man's power nor an easy matter. Hence it is that such excellence is rare, praiseworthy and noble."
> - Aristotle
>
> "Education costs money, but then so does ignorance."
> - Sir Claus Moser

There is no question that an undergraduate education and medical school will be expensive for you. The average student can expect to graduate from medical school with $250,000 in debt. This will usually cover expenses of books, housing, and daily living expenses. Although the final cost may seem outrageously high, one must remember that the average physician today makes around $150,000 a year. Thus, one can confidently say that the final result will justify the years of investment.

If finances are an important issue for you, than the specific program you attend can dramatically make a difference in cost. It is important for you to become familiar with the different loans that you can receive to pay for your education. This chapter will serve as your definitive guide to be able to afford an accelerated medical program or any path you decide to take while in school. We have broken down the chapter by the subjects of loans, scholarships, and grants at the federal and state levels.

Federal Loans, Grants, and Scholarships

There are basically four types of loans a student can receive: private, institutional, state, and federal. Each university usually has a financial aid officer that can assist you in choosing the best loans for you. There are also several grants and scholarships at the federal and state level which a student can be awarded and does not have to pay back! Here is a list of the different types of federal loans one can take as a student.

NAGENDRA SAI KONERU, M.D.
VINEET ARORA, M.D.
OMAR WANG, ATC

1) **Federal Student Stafford Loan (SSL):** This is a federal loan administered by a lender such as a bank. The maximum allocation is usually slightly over $18,000 a year. One must demonstrate financial need to be eligible. A student will receive 10 years to pay off the Stafford loan. The advantage to this loan is that interest will not begin until after graduation. Payment usually is initiated 6 months after graduation. The maximum interest charged is no more than 8.5%.

Advantages: Interest does not accrue until after graduation. The best type of loan a student can receive.
Disadvantages: Low cumulative allocation.

2) **Unsubsidized Stafford Student Loan:** This is a federal loan administered by a lender such as a bank. The maximum allocation is slightly over $18,000 a year.

Advantages: There are no eligibility requirements such as financial need.
Disadvantages: Interest accrues the day the loan is disbursed.

3) **Federal Supplemental Loan for Students (SLS):** This is a federal loan administered by a lender such as a bank. This is not a need based loan, but the student must first apply to the Federal Student Stafford Loan. The maximum allocation is usually $10,000 a year. A student will have 10 years to repay this loan.

Advantages: There is no eligibility requirements assuming one already applied for the SSL.
Disadvantages: There is a high interest rate which begins while the student is in school.

4) **Perkins Loan:** This is federal loan usually administered by the university the student is attending. The maximum allocation is usually no more than $5,000 per year with a cumulative maximum of $18,000. The student will have 10 years to repay the loan and payments can be deferred for a few years. There is usually a fixed interest payment of about 5%.

Advantages: Low interest rates for loan
Disadvantages: There is a low maximum cumulative allocation

Additional information on federal loans, grants, and scholarships:

1) **Guaranteed Student Loans:** This is a program sponsored by the U.S. department of education. The program objective is to approve loans for educational expenses from lenders such as banks, schools, credit unions, etc. There is over $9,000,000,000 available in this fund!
   Info: Guaranteed Student Loans Program
           Division of Policy Development
           Office of Assistant Secretary for Postsecondary Education

U.S. Department of Education
Washington D.C., 20202
Tel: 1-202-708-8242

2) **Programs of Excellence in Health Professions Education for Minorities**: This program was started by the U.S. government to strengthen the national capacity to support minority students going in to the health professions. There is about $23,000,000 allocated to this program!

> Info: Division of Disadvantaged Assistance
> Bureau of Health Professions
> Health Resources and Services Administration
> Public Health Service
> U.S. Department of Health and Human Services
> Room 8A-09, Parklawn Building
> 5600 Fishers Lane
> Rockville, MD 20857
> Tel: 1-301-443-4495

3) **Robert C. Byrd Honors Scholarships**: This program provides $1,500 per year to college students in the form of grants. The program provides scholarships to students who show promise of academic achievement. One must contact the State educational agency if interested. There is over $29,000,000 available in this programs fund!

> Info: U.S. Department of Education
> Office of Student Financial Assistance
> Office of the Assistant Secretary for Postsecondary Education
> Division of Higher Education Incentives Programs
> The Portals, Suite C-80
> Washington D.C., 20024
> Tel: 1-202-260-3394

4) **Federal Pell Grant Program:** This program is available for undergraduates who have demonstrated financial need. The program will provide up to $2300 per year in grants for students.
   Info: Division of Policy Development

Would you still like to have more information about Federal aid? You can receive a free application from the Federal Student Aid Information Center. You can receive a free application for federal student aid and copies of *The Student Financial Aid Handbook.*
   Info: Federal Student Aid Information Center
   P.O. Box 84
   Washington D.C., 20044
   Tel: 1-800-433-3243

NAGENDRA SAI KONERU, M.D.
VINEET ARORA, M.D.
OMAR WANG, ATC

State loans, grants, and scholarships

Did you know that there is over three billion dollars worth of money in state aid for students just like you?! After you have gone through all the federal programs and have found what is available for you, the next step is the to check your state to see what kinds of loans, grants, and scholarships are available. There are so many students who do not take advantage of this opportunity simply from lack of awareness.

For example, Alabama and New Mexico have grants available for any students attending a private university! North Carolina and New York have $1,500 grants for all undergraduate students who go to school full time! Oklahoma has scholarships that cover tuition, fees, and room and board for financially troubled students.

The government is literally giving away free money. We encourage you to use the numbers we provide in Appendix B to enquire about money that you can obtain through loans, grants, or scholarships at the state level.

THE HIGH SCHOOL DOCTOR
The Underground Roadmap to 6, 7, and 8 Year
Accelerated/Combined Medical Programs (BA/MD) in the United States

Medical School After High School? The Accelerated Medical Programs (BA/MD)

> "The rate and magnitude of change is such that the contents of a medical student, like the contents of a text-book, are partly out of date at the time of publication. Indeed, I've made a little speech to fourth year students that runs like this: 'Your teachers have tried to give you a good opportunity to learn and to offer you information which the evidence indicated to be accurate. Nevertheless, probably half of what you know is no longer true. This troubles me, but what troubles me more is that I don't know which half it is.'"
>
> -C. Sidney Burwell, the dean of Harvard Medical School from 1935 to 1949

You have probably all heard about these programs, whether it be from friends, parents, or teachers. However, no other source will provide an easy to follow detailed discussion concerning this topic than that presented in this chapter. Accelerated medical programs are programs which offer high school seniors the ability to have a conditional seat in a medical school. Some of these programs are offered to sophomores in college and are often labeled as "early assurance" programs. Whatever the case may be, these programs offer an early admission into medical school, saving time and stress for the college student. We will attempt to clarify the following major questions about these programs:

What is the purpose of such programs?
What characteristics are the programs seeking in applicants?
Are these programs right for you?
How do you choose the correct program — a summary of all of
the U.S. Programs?

NAGENDRA SAI KONERU, M.D.
VINEET ARORA, M.D.
OMAR WANG, ATC

What is the purpose of the accelerated medical Program?

In understanding a task such as applying to a BA/MD program, you must consider the goal of such programs. An admissions counselor might say that often medical schools offer these combined programs as a recruiting tool, in order to attract top high school students who otherwise would not have considered that medical school. The basis for that statement is that these top high school students would have gone the traditional route and chosen to attend the top medical schools in the nation.

By employing accelerated programs, schools that are of slightly lower reputation are able to contend with the top tier medical schools by recruiting and winning the "cream of the crop." Another reason that schools may offer such programs if for the fact that you will be an investment for them. In agreeing to enroll you in the program, they are ensuring a solid six to eight years of tuition payments, and creating doctors that will give back more money to the program as alumni.

What characteristics are the programs seeking in applicants?

For the most part, these programs are geared to attract the most highly qualified high school seniors with a strong desire to pursue medicine as a career. These programs are not easy to gain admission to. You will be judged with other qualified applicants on your GPA, standardized test scores, leadership and service activities, research, and your commitment to enter medicine as your main playing fields.

Every candidate will probably have excellent credentials, so our advice is, in addition to the above categories, try to distinguish yourself with unusual talents or credits. For instance, a national debate champion or a prodigy musician are two such distinguishing talents. To further explore what characteristics these programs are looking for, see the sample vignettes in the next chapter.

Are These Programs Right For You? *Things to consider ...*

Are you absolutely sure you want to be a physician?

In considering whether such combined programs are right for you, the most important thing that must be present is a strong motivation to enter medicine. In today's age, it is fairly easy to be enticed by the medical profession. It is traditionally one associated with prestige, job security, and a sizable amount of money in the bank. Television shows such as E.R. do a very nice job of glamorizing the profession. However, you must be able to view yourself as a decision to be sure of while only sixteen or seventeen years old.

You may think that you know you want to become a doctor, but do you really know what it is like? To be sure, it would be a great benefit to find out what a doctor and medical student's life is really like from a wide variety of sources. Seek out a student at an accelerated/guaranteed program and ask questions. In addition, talk to pre-meds who are going the more traditional route at a state university or private college. And most importantly, talk to a doctor. A good idea would be to follow or shadow the doctor in his/her duties for the day.

Reputation of the college associated with the accelerated medical program

This is a critical factor in your decision because you are limiting your career choices from the beginning — should you change your mind about medicine or decide you may be interested in another career, there are drawbacks to already being enrolled in such a track program. To illustrate this, consider the following scenario: you are enrolled in the accelerated/guaranteed program and sometime during your undergrad years, for whatever reason (lack of interest, curiosity of another profession, too many frat parties leave you with a severe dent in your GPA and the school is kicking you out of the program because you didn't maintain the requirements), you decide to leave the program and just get a bachelor's degree. However, the engineering or liberal arts major that you want to pursue is not offered at this school.

Perhaps the school is a large state university with a great support system for the accelerated/guaranteed program, but very little for making the regular undergraduate feel like not just another number. In any case, back to today, you are a bright student and can probably choose to get your bachelor's from a top university.

So, the question to ask yourself is whether you are interested in attending the college/university associated with the accelerated/guaranteed program should you no longer be in that program. If the answer is yes, great — but if you're not sure that the school is the right choice for you and the only draw is the program, THINK CAREFULLY because you are essentially locking yourself in a decision that hinges that you complete the program.

Social atmosphere in the program

While this may sound like something that doesn't really matter to you because the only thing you care about is attending the program or because you are confident that you can make friends anywhere, a word of advice is to check this out carefully. Depending on the program you select, you might be choosing a road very different from the normal college experience — friends of all sorts of interests and majors, the indecision that helps you grow and mature as a college student.

Some programs may be more inntegrated with the undergraduate school than others, so the experience of attending a normal college is retained. However, in some cases, students in the accelerated/guaranteed programs are isolated in a dorm and take all the same classes together, which can equal a very strange experience since these programs can last up to eight years. Are you prepared for that fate if you don't get along so well with your class? Thus, in choosing the correct program you should visit each school, the location around the school, inquire about the housing program, social contact with the other undergraduate students, and the number of students in the program. Seek the opinion of people within the program itself.

Medical school associated with the accelerated program

You are selecting the medical school that you will be attending from a very early point in your career. Typically, most students decide which medical school they wish to apply to and attend in their final two years of college. Your first instincts may be to apply to the programs that seem like the best undergrad program for you, but the most lifetime investment comes from the M.D. degree. Consider the fact that your M.D. degree is going to be coming from that particular medical school and the implications on your future.

NAGENDRA SAI KONERU, M.D.
VINEET ARORA, M.D.
OMAR WANG, ATC

For example, is the medical school primarily concerned with comprehensive care or is it a research oriented school? How do the students do on the board exams? Do most students get residencies of their top choice? Once again, talking to someone at a particular program will provide invaluable insights on your decision.

Time course of the program

One of the major differences among the programs is the time course of the programs. As you probably know, some programs offer attractive accelerated programs that cut down on the number of years it takes to complete the M.D. However, the years that are cut down are the undergraduate years. There are obvious advantages (you are not 30 by the time you have your M.D.), but also, not so obvious disadvantages.

For example, the undergraduate years that are cut can be viewed as disadvantageous in a few ways. One, the accelerated programs usually merit summers spent studying, as well as generally a more rigorous course load per semester to finish everything early. This may not be an attractive option for those of you who don't wish to subject yourself to such stress.

In addition, the accelerated programs don't offer much time for liberal arts studies or pursuits of outside interests during the undergraduate years which is usually a big part of most students' lives. When looking back on college, many doctors may think of opportunities they had taken to explore the humanities such as philosophy, writing studies, or art which have developed into hobbies which they now love. However, in some of these accelerated programs, you may not have time or the ability to explore these hobbies.

Location, location, location!!!

This may sound ridiculous, but this weighs about equal weight with the other factors involved in choosing an accelerated/guaranteed program. You are about to spend the most crucial years of your life in one pace – your choice should be one that you can live with. Points to consider are if you are the kind of person who is fairly independent and would not mind living far away from home for long periods of time.

Perhaps you attended boarding school for high school and living away from home is something not foreign. However, for most of you, going away will be a very exciting and challenging experience. Because the pressures of medical school itself can be quite demanding, some students choose a program close to home so that a weekend trip home to get away is not completely inconceivable or out of budget.

Other things to consider are if you prefer to live in a big city or in a university town. Not only does this impact on your social events and life, but also on your medical education. A hospital in a big city is more likely to have a diverse patient population and more facilities as a teaching hospital. You will find that many states medical colleges are not associated with the college town, but are in the big city for this very reason — to provide a better medical education.

Another point to keep in mind is that this program is not going to be easy. At least if you enjoy the place that you study, you can keep your piece of mind. For instance, if you grew up in a city, perhaps attending an accelerated program in a rural area is not such a good idea. Most likely, your ideal location is a sunny beach in California, however, this may not be one of the choices that you end up with.

The question is can you be happy where you are. Considering that medical students are a population known to be afflicted with depression more than the general population, this is a serious matter. Having a support group consisting of non medical friends, family, and being able to study in a comfortable environment are all things that are advantages of going to a school near home. You must decide what is right for you.

NAGENDRA SAI KONERU, M.D.
VINEET ARORA, M.D.
OMAR WANG, ATC

Chapter 5

The Standardized Tests

> *Do not worry about your difficulties in mathematics, I assure you that mine are greater.*
>
> *- Albert Einstein*

The two most common standardized tests are the SAT and the ACT. Many have argued that the test is not an accurate predictor of how one will perform in college, and that it can be culturally or racially biased. Like it or not though – these tests are here to stay.

Standardized tests are valuable in that they provide a medium for students of all backgrounds from all over the world to be compared. No single test can prove one's intelligence or how good of a doctor one will be; nevertheless some form of standardized test is necessary. It is impossible to judge students solely on the G.P.A. Is a G.P.A. of 3.5 that includes many AP courses more impressive than a G.P.A. of 4.0 that is comprised of less demanding coursework? Is a G.P.A. of 3.7 in a small public school in Iowa the same as a G.P.A. of 3.7 in a private school in Los Angeles?

As you can see there can be so many situations that can arise that could lead to misleading results solely based on a student's G.P.A., that's where the standardized tests come into play.

Scholastic Aptitude Test (SAT)

The Scholastic Assessment Test, or the "S-A-T" as it is commonly called, is the most well known standardized test as it is a requirement in many colleges and universities around the country. The SAT is an aptitude test that measures a student's ability in English and Math.

Format of the SAT

The SAT is comprised of seven sections and a three-hour time limit. There is an "experimental" section so only 6 of the sections will comprise your score. Don't worry about the "experimental" section, as you will not know which one it is. Here is the sample format of what you can expect on the SAT.

Section: Type of Questions
Verbal
10 Sentence Completions
13 Analogies
30 minutes

12 Reading Comprehension

Verbal
9 Sentence Completions
6 Analogies
30 minutes

15 Reading Comprehension

Mini Verbal
13 Reading Comprehension
15 minutes

Math
25 Multiple-choice
30 minutes

Math
15 Quantitative Comparisons
30 minutes

10 Grid-ins
15 minutes

Mini Math
10 Mulitiple-choice
15 minutes

Experimental
Verbal or Math
30 minutes

Should I make sure to answer all the questions?

    Time is an important consideration when taking the SAT. Nothing can prepare you to learn how much time should be spent than taking multiple practice tests. Just like a marathoner paces himself and knows how fast he needs to go to make sure he/she has enough gas at the end, the same should be practiced and established before taking this test. Although time is strictly limited on the SAT, working too quickly can damage your score. Students are often conditioned to skim passages and get the general gist of what it's trying to say, however the SAT writers realize this and they throw in subtle points to throw you off. It is essential to carefully read the passages while paying critical attention to some of the finer points.

The SAT intentionally makes you struggle to answer every question, and one might rush through all the questions to reach the end. This approach however isn't a wise one. If you try to answer all the questions on this test quickly and without paying attention to detail, you are going to have a poor score. The key to gaining a good score on the SAT is answering a higher percentage of questions correct instead of frantically rushing through the entire test and making careless mistakes. Of course this doesn't mean that you should take a half an hour per question to make sure it's absolutely correct, but you should find a comfortable pace that lets you find the correct answer and thus an overall better score.

1600?

I'm sure everyone has heard of someone boasting about getting a 1600 on the SAT. What does that mean? Well, as mentioned earlier there are two parts of the test, English and Math. Both parts are scored independently, and each section has a range from 200-800. Thus a 1600 would be a perfect score. Still confused? If so, maybe med school isn't for you.

The answer is...C, no B, no it's probable A or D

Students often times are faced with questions in which they are clueless. Some questions on the SAT are extremely difficult. Some students take it as a personal challenge and refuse to give up on it. If this was cancer research, I want that kind of student. However, remember you are on a time constraint and one question isn't going to make or brake you. To get a high score, you must learn when to just move on to the next question. All questions are of equal value, regardless of how difficult they are. So if you are struggling with a particular question, move on...this isn't a test on persistence.

To Guess or Not to Guess

There is a small penalty for incorrect answers on the SAT, but in our opinion a larger penalty for blank answers. Many times students are torn between two or maybe three choices in which case the percentages are in your favor to make an educated guess. Some mathematicians even claim that you should guess even if you can't eliminate one of the answers because the reward for getting a correct answer is substantially greater than a penalty for an incorrect one.

Order of Difficulty

If you are completely strapped for time try to answer the questions at the beginning of sections or new passages. The first few questions are generally easier as the questions increase in difficulty throughout a particular passage or section. Again, by taking practice tests you will see this trend and will learn to pace yourself and understand what kind of questions to expect where.

Helpful Hints

It is significantly harder to create an answer that seems almost right than it is to produce the correct answer. For this reason, there are usually only two possible choices; it's your task to find them. Often times the situation will arise when you are torn between two answers that both seem correct. Well, whatever you do make sure you make an educated guess on one of them.

The SAT question makers can usually produce one answer that seems misleading, but the other wrong answers are just usually words to fill the page. In essence, if you can flush out the three apparent incorrect answers you have increased your chances of success from 20% to 50%.

More Informational Sites on the SAT

The Educational Testing Service Network (www.ets.org)
Scholastic Testing Systems (www.testprep.com)
College Board (www.collegeboard.com)
Improve Sat Math scores (www.satmath.com)
Secrets of the SAT (http://www.pbs.org/wgbh/pages/frontline/shows/sats/)

American College Testing (ACT)

Don't make the mistake of thinking the SAT and ACT are similar tests! The SAT is an aptitude test while the ACT is an achievement test. The ACT Assessment® is more focused on finding out about your general educational development and your ability to complete college-level work.

Format of the ACT

The ACT Assessment, or "A-C-T" as it is commonly called, is a national college admission examination that consists of tests in:

English
Mathematics
Reading
Science Reasoning

The breakdown of the test is as follows:

1. English (75 questions, 45 minute test)
   a. Usage/Mechanics
      i. Punctuation (13%)
      ii. Basic Grammar and Usage (16%)
      iii. Sentence Structure (24%)
   b. Rhetorical Skills
      i. Strategy (16%)
      ii. Organization (15%)
      iii. Style (16%)
2. Math (60 questions, 60 minute test)

a. Pre-Algebra/Elementary Algebra
    i. Pre-Algebra (23%)
    ii. Elementary Algebra (17%)
b. Intermediate Algebra/Coordinate Geometry
    i. Intermediate Algebra (15%)
    ii. Coordinate Geometry (15%)
c. Plane Geometry/Trigonometry
    i. Plane Geometry (23%)
    ii. Trigonometry (7%)
3. Reading (40 questions, 35 minute test)
    a. Social Studies (25%)
    b. Natural Sciences (25%)
    c. Prose Fiction (25%)
    d. Humanities (25%)
4. Science Reasoning (40 questions, 35 minute test)
    a. Data Representation (38%)
    b. Research Summaries (45%)
    c. Conflicting Viewpoints (17%)

ACT Scoring

The ACT Assessment score is calculated in the following manner: your number of correct answers are counted, and are then converted to scale scores that have the same meaning for all the tests. The scale scores range from 1 (low) to 36 (high) for each of the four tests and for the Composite. The Composite is the average of your four test scores, rounded to the nearest whole number.

Shall I Guess?

There are absolutely no penalties for incorrect answers, so even if you find yourself at the end of a section with numerous blanks, fill them all in.

Underground Tips

Again, the best preparation for this type of test is to practice, practice, practice. We can't preach this enough, because this is the only way you are going to get comfortable with the length, type of questions, and difficulty. If you find you are particularly weak in an area you can target this and help boost your score. There are also sorts of practice kits and study guides with helpful hints you can obtain. We have tried to list some of these sources at the end of this section.

Is the ACT Necessary?

The ACT isn't absolutely necessary for some colleges but it is something you might want to consider if an assessment test is more catered to your test-taking skills. The ACT Assessment tests are universally accepted for college admission, including all of the Ivy League schools.

Again, the ACT Assessment is not an IQ test so it bases its' questions on subject matter you have learned throughout your schooling. Most students find this test to their liking as opposed to the SAT, which is an aptitude test.

Another option that the ACT Assessment provides is a chance for a student to gain insight for future career and educational planning. The student profile assessment helps highlight some of your strengths and areas that might need some improvement. This could prove as an invaluable tool in future endeavors.

Another great advantage of this test is that you may retake it as many times as you wish. Also, you control what scores are sent to prospective colleges. So whether you were feeling sick on test day, misunderstood something, or just had an anxiety attack, don't worry you will have another chance.

More Informational Sites on the ACT
ACT'S HOMEPAGE (www.act.org)
ACT/SAT Test Prep (http://www.go-student.com/)
ACT Made Easy (http://www.actmadeeasy.com/)
Test Prep (http://www.ivy.com/ivyfaq.asp)
Resource Center for ACT (http://www.testinfo.net/act.htm)

NAGENDRA SAI KONERU, M.D.
VINEET ARORA, M.D.
OMAR WANG, ATC

Chapter 6

The *Underground* Timetable for High School Students

> *If I had to sum up in one word what makes a good manager, I'd say decisiveness. You can use the fanciest computers to gather the numbers, but in the end you have to set a timetable and act.*
> -Lee Iacocca

Creating a timeline for yourself will prove to be one of the most important and valuable decisions of your admission strategy. The stress can be overwhelming for you if you don't have a clear and concise plan from the beginning. Most importantly, creating a timeline will give you a tremendous edge over other students because it will help you visualize the tasks that you need to do in order to become the best possible candidate for an accelerated medical program. Here is an underground timetable which we feel will give you a competitive edge over the rest!

FRESHMAN YEAR

- Enroll in the classes that are designed to prepare you for college and the standardized exams.
- Set up at least 4 appointments with your high school counselor, preferably in the early fall and spring, to schedule your classes and to discuss your desire to go into an accelerated medical program.
- Begin looking into programs for the summer that you can join.
- Start buying SAT and ACT review books.
- Build your vocabulary by reading books, journals, and literary magazines.
- Start looking for volunteering opportunities at your local hospital or other area of need.
- Join school activities and sports of your choice.

SOPHOMORE YEAR

- Enroll in the classes that are designed to prepare you for college and the standardized exams.
- Make appointments in October and January with your counselor to discuss the status of your classes and GPA.
- Ask counselors to post College Day/College Night schedules and look for the associated undergraduate universities with accelerated medical programs.
- Continue the organizations and clubs that you joined during your freshman year.

JUNIOR YEAR

- Study the admission requirements for the accelerated medical programs that interest you. Check that you are taking appropriate courses to meet college entrance requirements.
- Meet with your counselor and mentors.
- Examine possible financial aid or college admissions meetings held in your region.
- Register for and take the Preliminary Scholastic Aptitude Test (PSAT) and the National Merit Scholarship Qualifying Test (NMSQT), usually given in October.
- Think about people who would be good candidates to write you a recommendation; start with teachers, counselors and employers.
- In the spring, register for the Scholastic Aptitude Test (SAT), Achievement Test, or the American College Test (ACT).
- See your counselor about available Summer Enrichment Programs. We have provided you a list of resources in our appendix.

SENIOR YEAR

July and August

- Write the accelerated medical programs via the postcards that are provided for in our appendix. Visit selected college campuses; talk to graduates and students at the institutions.

September

- Maintain or improve academic grades. College officials don't like to see slipping grades.
- Check with your counselor to determine which tests are required and the deadlines for applying.
- Set up a calendar for taking tests and completing college applications.

- Make sure to fulfill application requirements.
- Check early-decision deadlines. See your counselor when you have questions and need help.

October and November

- Attend College Day/Night programs.
- Apply to colleges and accelerated medical programs with different admission requirements (least selective to more selective). Make sure that you have some backup colleges that you know that you will definitely be accepted into. Acceptance into an accelerated medical program can be quite unpredictable even if you are well qualified.
- Ask your counselor to look over your application form and discuss the next steps in applying to the accelerated medical programs.
- See your counselor about completing the Financial Aid Form (FAF). Colleges require that students requesting financial aid provide the FAF, including the part that explains any unusual financial circumstances.
- Check for testing deadlines and scholarship information.
- Mail completed forms to colleges.
- Check Military Academy and ROTC application and scholarship deadlines if appropriate.

December

- Send all applications and copies of high school grades to the colleges before Christmas, unless a college indicates otherwise.
- Give your guidance counselor all required forms at least two weeks before they are due since November and December are very busy months for counselors.
- Take the Achievement Test required by some colleges.
- Write thank you notes for everyone that has written you recommendations.

January

- Mail the Financial Aid Form (FAF).
- Some colleges accept outstanding candidates during this month.
- Take the College Board Achievement Tests if required by the colleges and if you have not taken them previously.

February

- Ask your counselor to send your first semester's grades to the colleges, along with any other information not already forwarded. Some colleges provide forms for this purpose and some do not.

March

- Recheck college catalogs and see your counselor to make sure that you have taken all of the necessary tests. If you haven't, make sure you register to take the tests in May.

April, May and June

- Keep a record of acceptances, rejections, and financial aid awards.
- Reply promptly to the accelerated medical program to notify them of your decision.
- Reply promptly when you are notified that you have been awarded a financial aid package.
- Tell the college whether you are accepting or refusing the award.
- Meet the reply deadline or you may lose the admission acceptance or financial aid you have earned.
- Before you leave school in June, see your counselor to request that a final transcript be sent to the college or university of your choice.

THINGS TO SAVE

- Copies of guidance office newsletters
- Cancelled checks or money order receipts
- Admission tickets to tests and correction forms
- All test score reports
- Transcripts of high school grades
- Work copy of the FAF and all other financial aid forms
- College Scholarship Services acknowledgment form
- Copies of all correspondence sent to or received from schools, including applications and acceptances.

NAGENDRA SAI KONERU, M.D.
VINEET ARORA, M.D.
OMAR WANG, ATC

The Underground High School Vignettes

> *"When we walk to the end of all the light we have,
> and take a step into the darkness of the unknown,
> we must believe one of two things will happen:
> that we will land on something solid,
> or we will learn to fly."*
> **unknown**

High School Vignettes

Scenario 1:

David DOE. SAT score: 1200 (650 math, 550 verbal), ACT score: 27; High School GPA: 3.5 (top 10% of class); hospital volunteer 2 years; newspaper 1 year; cross country 2 years.

David would not be competitive enough to qualify for 90% of the accelerated/guaranteed programs. Unfortunately, the ones he did qualify for, he probably would not be called for an interview. Although his GPA is not bad, his extracurricular activities are not outstanding enough to pull him through for any attention. None of his activities reflect any type of commitment or dedication. David should probably not waste too much energy on accelerated/guaranteed programs.

Scenario 2:

Kal DOE. SAT score 1500 (750 math, 750 verbal), ACT: 33; High School GPA: 3.9 (top 2% of class); no activities.

Kal has a shining academic record with great scores on his standardized test scores. This proves that Kal is a great test taker. But what else do we know about Kal? He will fulfill all the requirements with flying colors for all of the accelerated/guaranteed programs, and he will most likely be called for an interview. However, since he has no activities to speak of, he will fall behind all the other well-rounded applicants.

Scenario 3:

Omar DOE. SAT score 1350 (700 math, 650 verbal), ACT score: 30: High School GPA: 3.6 (top 5% of class); newspaper 4 years (editor 1 year), tennis 4 years (State qualifier); Math Team 4 years; hospital volunteer 4 years; National Honor Society.

Omar does not have outstanding standard test scores or an outstanding GPA; however, his application would fulfill the minimum requirements for most programs. What really puts Omar in the race is the fact that he is actively involved in organizations and clubs. He shows commitment by having prolonged participation in all of the activities. What might bring Omar to the finish line and get him an interview is the fact that he is a tennis prodigy.

Scenario 4:

Kim DOE. SAT score 1480 (750 math, 630 verbal), ACT score: 32; High School GPA: 3.85 (top 3% of class); Red Cross volunteer 3 years; hospital volunteer 4 years; Argonne National Labs 2 summers; volleyball 4 years (team captain 2 years); newspaper 4 years.

Kim has a complete resume. Not only does she have a solid academic profile, but she also shows commitment, leadership, and compassion in her activities. Kim has a great chance of getting an interview for an accelerated/guaranteed program.

NAGENDRA SAI KONERU, M.D.
VINEET ARORA, M.D.
OMAR WANG, ATC

The Underground Résumé

> *The life of every man is a diary in which he means to write one story, and writes another.*
>
> –James Matthew Barrie

Why Write A Resume During High School?

Writing a resume can be very helpful during high school. First of all, it will teach you how to become proficient at resume writing – an asset that you will need later in your career. Second, it will be important when you start asking people to write you letters of recommendation. Anyone who is writing you a letter will greatly appreciate a resume for it will save them time and it will let them write a more thorough letter. Finally, it will help you during your interview preparation, since it will provide you quick and easy access to your major accomplishments.

We strongly recommend that you use your school's library or career center in finding information about writing powerful resumes. If your school's center is lacking with resume resources than a public library or a major bookstore will do. We have provided some sample resumes that are fantastic. You do not need to follow one of these structures identically but it should aid you in developing your own.

Sample Resume

Sarita Doe
1923 Adams Street
Chicago, IL 31204
(555) 742-2783
Email: Sarita_Doe@hotmail.com

EDUCATION

HOFFMAN ESTATES HIGH SCHOOL — Hoffman Estates, IL

- High School Diploma Candidate, June 2002
- GPA 3.8/4.0
- Ranked 20 out of 500 students in my senior class

High School Courses Taken

AP Economics	AP U.S. History
AP English	AP Biology
AP Calculus I & II	AP Physics
AP Chemistry	AP German

ACTIVITIES

HIGH SCHOOL TENNIS TEAM — Hoffman Estates, IL

- Two years as team captain
- IHSA Men's Tennis State Qualifier in the spring of 2001
- Placed top 30 in the state of Illinois
- ATP ranked

HIGH SCHOOL MATH TEAM — Hoffman Estates, IL

- Treasurer for the past three years
- Contributed to the top ten finish at the Illinois state championships

NAGENDRA SAI KONERU, M.D.
VINEET ARORA, M.D.
OMAR WANG, ATC

BARRINGTON HOSPITAL — S. Barrington, IL

- Worked as a volunteer since August 2000
- Assisted the physicians with the care of injured patients that came into the ER

ARGONNE NATIONAL LABS — Argonne, IL

- Did an internship during summer of 2001. Studied principles of electrophotometry.
- Was Published in the Journal of Electrophotometry Vol 12 Nov 2001.

SOUP KITCHEN VOLUNTEER — Schaumburg, IL

- Volunteer since August 2000.
- Served and cooked various dishes to the homelss

HONORS

- National Honor Society (3 years)
- Who's Who in the United States 2000
- National Merit Semifinalist

SKILLS

- American Red Cross First Aid, Certified from 1994-Present
- American Red Cross CPR, Certified from 1994-Present
- MT Certified, Training completed May 1999

REFERENCES

Charles Swanik, Ph.D., ATC
Head of the Science Department
Hoffman Estates High School
1000 JD Anderson Drive
Philadelphia, PA 19122
(999) 204-9555

Dr. John Spiker
Neurosurgeon
Barrington Hospital
S. Barrington, IL 60010
(999) 599-2515

Randy Dicksmack
Head Tennis Coach
Hoffman Estates High School
P.O. Box 0877
Morgantown, WY 26507
(999) 293-2737 ext. 1

John Smith
Argonne National Labs
Research Division
1000 South Allen
Argonne, IL 66720
(999) 424-152

THE HIGH SCHOOL DOCTOR
The Underground Roadmap to 6, 7, and 8 Year
Accelerated/Combined Medical Programs (BA/MD) in the United States

Chapter 9

Letters of Recommendation

> *"There are two kinds of people, those who do the work and those who take the credit. Try to be in the first group; there is less competition there."*
> — *Indira Gandhi*

College applications will generally require you to have two to three letters of recommendation from people who you have had contact with inside or outside the classroom. The letters of recommendation that you get can literally make the difference between an acceptance letter or a rejection.

Who are the right people to ask?

Imagine being on the admissions committee of an accelerated medical program. Who's letters are going to be weighted more than others? First and foremost, we stress the importance of substance. It doesn't matter if you get a letter from a physician if you only saw him 3 times. However, a heartfelt letter from your volunteer coordinator or tennis coach whom you worked with for four years can serve as gold. The important tip to remember is that the actual content of the letter weighs much more weight than by whom it is from.

When should I ask?

The more time you give someone, the more time they can spend on writing a letter of depth about you. A good time frame would be at least one month before the letters are actually due. Check the application deadlines for the specific programs that you are applying for to decide the exact time to give your requests.

How can I make sure that I get the best possible recommendations?

Be honest with your recommender. Tell them that you want to go to an accelerated medical program. Inform them how competitive these programs are, and more importantly, tell them what these programs are looking for in a candidate – the qualities of the ideal physician.

NAGENDRA SAI KONERU, M.D.
VINEET ARORA, M.D.
OMAR WANG, ATC

Providing the recommenders with a resume will help them know specific goals and interests that you may have. We have provided a chapter on resume writing in the next chapter. Tell them to be as specific as possible about you. The best resumes are the ones that use specific examples and stories.

Underground Tip #1:
Do not be shy to ask for a good recommendation. Teachers and mentors often feel honored that you are asking them.

Underground Tip #2:
Waive your right to see the recommendation letters. This will show the admissions committee that you have nothing to hide.

Underground Tip #3:
Make sure that you follow up with your recommender in about 2-3 weeks to remind them of the deadline. Write thank you notes to all of the recommenders for taking time to write for you.

The Personal Statement

> 'To get the right word in the right place is a rare achievement. To condense the diffused light of a page of thought into the luminous flash of a single sentence, is worthy to rank as a prize composition just by itself...Anybody can have ideas—the difficulty is to express them without squandering a quire of paper on an idea that ought to be reduced to one glittering paragraph."
> -Mark Twain

So you have a high G.P.A. and a decent SAT/ACT score, what is going to distinguish you from the numerous students across the country with similar achievements? Welcome to your first interview – the paper interview, or more commonly called "the personal statement." This is your chance to highlight your accomplishments, experiences, and potential. The advantage of the personal statement as opposed to an in person interview is that you have complete control in writing your statement. You have time to formulate a strategy and to focus on the areas you would like the Admissions Committee to notice. You have as much time to shed light on your character and achievements and to separate yourself from others who are all vying for the select few spots in the accelerated medical schools.

Here is a strategy that the authors found to be successful in their personal statements:

Brainstorming

Describe yourself. What are your strengths/weaknesses? What have you done to combat any weaknesses that you might have? What motivates you? What type of situations do you thrive in?

Describe Accomplishments. What are your hobbies? What type of extra-curricular activities are you involved in? Think of situations in which you worked extremely hard. How have you handled stressful situations or difficult times in your life?

NAGENDRA SAI KONERU, M.D.
VINEET ARORA, M.D.
OMAR WANG, ATC

Describe future goals. What do you aspire to do? How do you go about obtaining your dreams/goals? How is this particular school going to aid in your career development?

Answering The Question

Usually there are facsimiles of three types of questions that you might be asked.

1. "Tell us about yourself?"
2. "Why do you want to attend our college/university?"
3. A creative question, such as "If you could invite three people to dinner, who would they be and why?" or "Explain a time in which you busted your tail, and failed, what did you learn from that experience?"

This is where the brainstorming strategy will help you answer these types of questions. You have the opportunity to focus on certain aspects that you want the Admissions Committee to notice. It's important to be concise and clear, the committee has several essays to read and they will notice stories that are interesting, well written, and to the point. Once you have an idea of the attributes you want in your essay it's time to choose a story.

Choosing A Story

Here it is important to write about an experience that will grab the reader's attention. It doesn't have to be earth shattering or glamorous just one that will provide the reader with insightful knowledge about you. Great personal statements are the ones in which a story ties in all the attributes, skills, goals that you want to personify. So the object is to explain to the reader these wonderful things about you in an interesting and creative manner. Remember, most admission committee members spend a couple of minutes reading this sample that you have spent hours on. So it is vital that you grab their attention and sustain their interest throughout the personal statement. Be original, thought provoking and concise.

We have provided you with a sample essay that actually worked. The anonymous student was accepted into an accelerated medical program.

Sample Essay

The sky is almost brown as the dust from the streets sweeps into the sky with no sharp horizon visible. Through the dust, I see a mesh of people in white garb staring at every passerby in the airport. With visible hesitation, I step closer to the crowd. Simultaneously, with a burst of elation and a sigh of relief, I hear my name shouted out by two strangers. Rushing to greet them, I examine their faces to unveil a slight resemblance to my own. These are the first cousins who I have never known. As I step into their car, I am eager to inspect every nook of their world. While extending my head outside the white dust covered Volkswagen bug, I catch my first glimpse of the land that paradoxically, I have never visited but is my past, India.

Eight weeks later and a world away, I am recounting the endless stories about meeting relatives, touring ancient temples, and working in a Punjab government hospital delivering babies in scorching 120 degree suites. Eventually, my mother's objections to this trip were replaced with praise for my independence and versatility. My father respected my decision to search for something I never truly understood, my heritage. My brother, in typical sibling jest, asked me what I brought for him. As he looked on curiously, I rummaged through my baggage and pulled a videotape of my travels. If he could not go with me, the least I could do is to bring some of India to him.

My mother always fantasized about my life as a famous neurosurgeon or neurologist, perhaps one day uncovering the key to my brother's condition, spina bifida. For me, it is questioning the pathophysiology of his condition that spurred my initial interest in a career in medicine. My interest has been intensified throughout high school as I learn more about human physiology. During my first year as an emergency medicine volunteer, I wondered in amazement as our preceptor elicited affirmative responses to a series of seemingly unrelated symptoms such as shortness of breath, pain in the chest, swelling of the ankles, and urinating in the middle of the night. After the patient session, as she explained the symptoms of the newly learned abbreviation "CHF", I entertained a career in internal medicine.

In a few short months, with visible hesitation, I step into the mailroom of our apartment at home and take my seat. With a simultaneous burst of elation and streak of trepidation, I see my name written on the front of the page. Rushing to the front my door, I do not stop to examine the faces of my parents, waiting with the anxious disposition we all share. Extending my hand to accept the official white envelope, I break the seal to catch my first glimpse of the unknown typewritten destination that I will be arriving at in a few short months, my future.

NAGENDRA SAI KONERU, M.D.
VINEET ARORA, M.D.
OMAR WANG, ATC

The Interview and the Thank You Letter

> *Whenever you give an interviewer a fact give him another fact that will contradict it. Then he'll go away with a jumble that he can't use at all.*
> *- Mark Twain's Speeches, " The Robert Fulton Fund"*

If you have made it this far, then you are in good shape. You have passed all of the preliminary screening and you are on even ground with the rest of the applicant pool. This is where you have to be remembered. If you are averse to public speaking, we highly recommend taking a speech class during school. In addition, get involved in clubs and activities where you will need to speak to others. An interview at an accelerated program is comparable to an interview at a medical school. In fact, most interviews are held at the medical school of the program itself. Thus, there are several preparations you must make before the interview. After the Interview, you must remember to follow up on the program!! The only way that a program director will remember your name and face is when you call or write back and express your gratitude and genuine interest in them. We have provided a sample thank you letter at the end of this chapter.

Underground Tip #1

Be up to date on what is going on in the medical community. Talk to physicians about current issues of health care. Read newspapers about the current trends in medicine. Talk to medical students about issues they are dealing with.

Underground Tip #2

Research the medical school you are being interviewed at. See if the school primarily focuses on research or clinical medicine.

Underground Tip #3

Be CONFIDENT. The interview is all about presenting and selling yourself. If you don't like yourself, why will the committee? You should walk into the interviewing room as you are the best candidate possible,

Underground Tip #4

Be proactive in the interview. After answering questions about yourself, ask the committee questions about the program. Ask thought-provoking questions. This will separate you from the others.

Underground Tip #5

Before the interview, take out your resume and review it. This is what the committee will be asking questions from. Make mental notes of important activities you have participated in and use them to talk about yourself.

Underground Tip #6

Be respectful and dress formally. This is a medical school interview, so don't wear jeans or a short skirt. The important thing to remember is to look polished and dignified. First impressions are all you may have.

Preparing for interviewing questions can be quite difficult. However, from our experience, most of the questions asked were friendly and benign. Some of these questions are placed here for possible worst case scenarios. We have found in these situations that honesty is the best possible solution. If you don't know the answer to the question, then tell the committee that you don't know. Trying to fabricate an answer will only get you into more trouble. If you are well prepared before the interview, you will have no shame, *even if you can't answer the question as you would have liked.* Here is a list of possible questions the selection committee might ask you:

What initiated your interest in medicine?

Maybe your parents are physicians. Was it a book that you read? Maybe a possible experience that you had when you were younger.

What do you feel about HMO's and their role in medicine?

Discuss the advantages and disadvantages of advantages of managed care. Talk about the importance of not neglecting quality of care for the patient while reducing overhead costs.

Why do you feel that you will be a good candidate for this program?

This is your chance to shine! Talk about your strengths.

Why would you like to attend this particular program?

Be honest.

NAGENDRA SAI KONERU, M.D.
VINEET ARORA, M.D.
OMAR WANG, ATC

What was your most rewarding experience as a hospital volunteer?
Another chance to shine! Talk in detail about a particular experience that shaped your impression on medicine.

What do you see doing with a medical degree?
A very open question. Don't tell the committee that you want to make a lot of cash money.

Why should our program accept you?
Similar to question number 3. Discuss your strengths with honesty

Describe some of your strengths and weaknesses.
Again, be honest!

What disadvantages do you see in pursuing medicine at such a young age? Advantages?
You can answer this question in many ways, all of which will vary according to your own personality.

Give one word that a peer would describe you as.
Talk to some friends and ask them what they see as your strengths.

What are your passions outside of school?
Music? Sports? Community Service? Endless possibilities….

Explain your low grade in _____
The best way to answer this is to be honest. However, don't tell the committee that you were out partying too hard that semester.

Tell me about your volunteering experience.
Another chance to shine!

What do you think is the most challenging issue of medicine today?
Managed care? The ethical issues of genetics research? Read some newspapers and magazines about the current state of medicine.

If you could find a cure for a particular disease, which one would it be and why?
Did you have a family member that passed away from a particular disease? There are hundreds of killer diseases such as cancer, AIDS, hepatitis, etc. that can be used. Relate one to a personal experience.

What do you think about condoms being given out freely in high schools?

Issues such as safe sexual practice and sexually transmitted diseases should be discussed. This question is a good example of the importance of reading journals and newspapers for knowledge of subject matter and important statistics.

What do you think about euthanasia?

There are hundreds of articles on euthanasia. Do your research and tell the committee how you honestly feel. There is no correct answer to this. However, remember the Hippocratic oath which says that physicians are to do no harm to their patients.

If an Amish individual comes to the hospital and refuses treatment based upon religion, and the treatment is his only hope, what would you do?

What more can you do than explain the consequences to the patient and family? If the answer is still no, than you must comply with the patients wishes.

What should a doctor's role be in the issue of abortion?

We are not going to touch this one…Just be honest.

Would you define a glass half empty or half full?

Always say half full! Be optimistic.

We didn't mean to frighten you with these questions, however, all of these questions were used at least once among the numerous students we got feedback from. The important thing to remember is that you need to treat this as a MEDICAL SCHOOL interview and not an undergraduate interview. The authors are confident that if the advice given above on preparation for the interview is followed, you will do just fine.

Sample Thank You Letter

Once the interview process is finished, the next step is the thank you letter. The follow-up for the interview can be just as important as the interview itself. The thank you letter shows the admissions committee that you are strongly interested in their program. Most high school students do not write thank you letters, but remembering that this interview is more reflective of a medical school interview will give you a definite advantage. We have proved a sample thank you letter in which you can model or alter to write your own.

NAGENDRA SAI KONERU, M.D.
VINEET ARORA, M.D.
OMAR WANG, ATC

January 20, 2001

Mark Baker, M.D.
Department of Internal Medicine
BA/MD Program Director
New York University School of Medicine
Hypertension Center
520 East 70th Street
New York, NY 10021

Dear Dr. Baker,

I would like to thank you for making my visit to the New York Hospital-Cornell Medical Center so enjoyable. I was especially impressed with the clinical teaching on attending rounds, the chief residents who led morning report, medicine grand rounds, and the facilities including the new hospital as well as the beautifully architectured ambulatory clinics. I am also very excited by the opportunity to live affordably in one of the most desirable regions in the country.

However, the most impressionable point of my interview day was the satisfaction voiced by all of the housestaff that I encountered. Of particular note, I had the opportunity to meet with Monika Shah and Karen Hart, former Washington University alumni and now residents in the internal medicine program. They assured me that I would be very happy and satisfied with the New York Hospital internal medicine training program. Because of all of these reasons and my strong desire live in New York, I plan to rank your program highly, and hope that my application will be considered accordingly.

Should you have any questions or need any additional information, please do not hesitate to call me at (314) 652-1631.

Sincerely,

Joseph Walters
Senior
Hoffman Estates High School

Chapter 12

THE AFTERMATH

> **Many of life's failures are people who did not realize how close they were to success when they gave up.**
> **— Thomas A. Edison**

Once you have completed your interview, just take some time to relax. You have done your best and that in itself is worth commendation. Remember that even if you don't get into the accelerated/guaranteed program, life does go on. If you have followed all our advice, your resume will still be capable of making you competitive with the most worthy institutions in the country. And remember that if you keep up the intensity that you started with, you will have no problem getting accepted into a medical school through the traditional route.

On the other hand, if you do find an acceptance letter in the mail, don't immediately jump and accept the tempting proposal. Remember all of the pros and cons that we have written to weigh your decision about the particular program. Look at each program that we will describe in the next chapters in detail. Look at all of the issues which may be important to you, such as tuition cost, undergraduate education, reputation of the program, and location. What if you get accepted into an ivy league school as well as an accelerated medical program? Now the decisions become more difficult. The answer lies within your desire to be a physician and how confident you are in your decision.

Remember that an accelerated program only makes it easier for you to get into medical school. If it has been your lifelong dream to attend Cornell or Princeton University which do not have accelerated programs, follow your dreams regardless. You can still get into medical school and you will fulfill your dreams of getting a quality education at an institution of your childhood desire.

NAGENDRA SAI KONERU, M.D.
VINEET ARORA, M.D.
OMAR WANG, ATC

Chapter 13

The Crème of The Crop: The Best Undergraduate and Medical School Programs

> *"Going to school as small as Emerson means that instead of saying, `Screw you Mr. 90803,` the administration will say, `Screw you, Joe.`"*
> – Joe B. -Emerson College
>
> *"Getting an education from MIT is like getting a drink from a firehose."*
> - Anonymous – MIT
>
> *"Contrary to popular belief, Cow Tipping is defiantly passé here."*
> - Anonymous - University of Connecticut

In this chapter we will give you several ranking of undergraduate schools along with some rankings of medical schools. The accelerated medical programs are ranked following the section on program profiles. Remember that our rank lists are biased towards our own preferences of what is important. We have utilized several sources such as the *Gourman Report* and *U.S. News and World Report*.

The Top 25 Undergraduate Universities

When ranking a university, there are several factors that one takes into account. One important factor is quality of education. Quality of education is decided by the faculty to student ratio, accessibility of faculty, and the resources on campus. Other considerations include the competitiveness of the student body which is generally decided by the average SAT scores of the incoming class as well as the low acceptance rate by the university among the pool of applicants. Here is a list of what we felt were the top 25 national universities:

Princeton University
Harvard University
Yale University
California Institute of Technology
Massachusetts Institute of Technology
Stanford University
University of Pennsylvania
Duke University
Dartmouth College
Columbia University
Cornell University
University of Chicago
Northwestern University
Rice University
Brown University
Johns Hopkins University
Washington University (St. Louis)
Emory University
University of California at Berkeley
University of Notre Dame
Vanderbilt University
Tufts University
University of Michigan at Ann Arbor
The College of William and Mary
New York University
University of North Carolina at Chapel Hill

The Top 25 Private Liberal Arts Colleges
Amherst College
Carleton College
Swarthmore College
Williams College
Wellesley College
Smith College
Pomona College
Washington and Lee University
Davidson College
Haverford College
Bowdoin College
Middlebury College
Grinnell College
Colgate College
Bates College

NAGENDRA SAI KONERU, M.D.
VINEET ARORA, M.D.
OMAR WANG, ATC

Hamilton College
Trinity College
College of the Holy Cross
Macalester College
Oberlin College
Vasser College
Bryn Mawr College
Whitman College
Union College
Colorado College

The Most Diverse National Universities

This list includes the national universities that have at least 30% of the student body comprised of minorities or other ethnicities besides Caucasian.
Rutgers University
University of California – Riverside
University of Houston
New Jersey Institute of Technology
University of Illinois – Chicago
University of California – Los Angeles
University of California – Berkeley
Stanford University
Rensselaer Polytechnic Institute
University of California – Davis
University of Miami
University of California – San Diego

The Most Diverse Private Liberal Arts Colleges
Occidental College
Whittier College
Wellesley College
Swarthmore College
Wesleyan College
Claremont College

The Best Medical Schools

It is very difficult to rank medical schools. In fact the American Association of Medical Colleges generally discourages one to follow any method of ranking. *U.S. News & World Report* does a yearly ranking of the best medical schools. The report usually divides medical schools by research focus or primary care focus. In other words, the medical schools are rated according to their research and their clinical training. The report is very useful. For example, if you decide that you are very clinically oriented, the schools which are ranked highly in primary care would be more beneficial to you. If you are more academically inclined and would like to find the latest anti-viral drug for HIV, than a medical school ranked highly on the research list would be important for you.

The Top 25 Medical Schools in Research
Harvard Unviersity
Johns Hopkins
Duke University
University of Pennsylvania
Washington University at St. Louis
Columbia University
University of California at San Francisco
Yale University
Stanford University
University of Michigan at Ann Arbor
Baylor University
Cornell University
University of Washington
University of California at Los Angeles
Vanderbilt University
Case Western Reserve University
University of Chicago
University of Texas at Dallas
Northwestern University
University of Pittsburgh
Emory University
Mount Sinai University
New York University
University of California at San Diego
University of North Carolina at Chapel Hill

The Top 25 Medical Schools in Primary Care
University of Washington
Oregon University
University of New Mexico
University of California at San Francisco
University of Massachusetts at Worcester
Michigan State University
University of North Carolina at Chapel Hill

NAGENDRA SAI KONERU, M.D.
VINEET ARORA, M.D.
OMAR WANG, ATC

University of Colorado
University of Iowa
University of Minnesota at Duluth
Harvard University
University of Missouri at Columbia
Case Western Reserve University
University of Rochester, NY
University of Wisconsin at Madison
East Carolina University
Johns Hopkins University
University of California at Davis
University of California at Los Angeles
Duke University
Southern Illinois University
Dartmouth Medical School
East Tennessee State University
SUNY at Stoney Brook
University of Michigan at Ann Arbor

THE HIGH SCHOOL DOCTOR
The Underground Roadmap to 6, 7, and 8 Year
Accelerated/Combined Medical Programs (BA/MD) in the United States

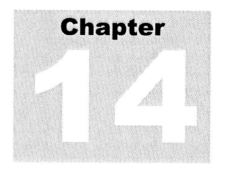

Accelerated Medical Program Listings

The spirit, the will to win, and the will to excel are the things that endure. These qualities are so much more important than the events that occur.
-Vince Lombardi

There are nearly 50 different accelerated/guaranteed medical programs in the country. We have provided you with a list of all the programs currently offered in the United States. Next, we have provided you with several profiles of programs which we are most familiar with. These programs vary from 6 to six- to eight-year medical programs. While most of the programs require that you be a senior in high school to apply, some programs will not take your application until your sophomore year in college.

Certain accelerated/guaranteed medical programs require that you do your undergraduate education at a different university than the associated medical school. This may be because the medical school may not have an associated undergraduate university. For example, Albany Medical College offers a program with three different undergraduate universities for the same program. Whatever the situation, it is important to do your research. The information given below should only be used as supplemental information. Since programs are constantly undergoing revisions, it is important for you to contact the school of choice for your ultimate reference guide. Also, keep your eyes open for new programs which are opening up every year.

We have listed the Medical schools throughout the United States by their associated State. The schools in bold are the medical schools offering conditional acceptance to high school students. The schools tagged next to the accelerated medical schools are the undergraduate components of each program.

ALABAMA
    University of Alabama
        University of Alabama
    University of South Alabama
        University of South Alabama

NAGENDRA SAI KONERU, M.D.
VINEET ARORA, M.D.
OMAR WANG, ATC

ARIZONA
University of Arizona
Midwestern University

ARKANSAS
University of Arkansas for Medical Sciences

CALIFORNIA
University of California-Davis
University of California-Irvine
University of California-Los Angeles
University of California-Riverside
University of California-San Diego
University of California-San Francisco
Loma Linda University
University of Southern California
University of Southern California
Stanford University

COLORADO
University of Colorado

CONNECTICUT
University of Connecticut
Yale University

DISTRICT OF COLUMBIA
George Washington University
George Washington University
Georgetown University
Howard University
Howard University

FLORIDA
University of Florida
University of Miami
University of Miami
University of South Florida
University of South Florida (not profiled)

THE HIGH SCHOOL DOCTOR
The Underground Roadmap to 6, 7, and 8 Year
Accelerated/Combined Medical Programs (BA/MD) in the United States

GEORGIA
Emory University
Medical College of Georgia
Mercer University
Morehouse

HAWAII
University of Hawaii

ILLINOIS
University of Chicago
Finch University of Health Sciences
Illinois Institute of Technology
University of Illinois-Chicago
University of Illinois-Chicago (not profiled)
Northwestern University
Northwestern University
Rush Medical College
Southern Illinois University

INDIANA
Indiana University

IOWA
University of Iowa

KANSAS
University of Kansas

KENTUCKY
University of Kentucky
University of Louisville

LOUISIANA
Louisiana State University in New Orleans
Louisiana State University in Shreveport
Tulane University

MARYLAND
Johns Hopkins University
University of Maryland
Uniformed Services University of the Health Sciences

NAGENDRA SAI KONERU, M.D.
VINEET ARORA, M.D.
OMAR WANG, ATC

MASSACHUSETTS
Boston University
> *Boston University*

Harvard University
University of Massachusetts
Tufts University
> *Tufts University*
> *Brandeis University*

MICHIGAN
Michigan State University
> *Michigan State University*

University of Michigan
> *University of Michigan*

Wayne State University

MINNESOTA
Mayo Medical School
University of Minnesota (Duluth)
University of Minnesota (Minneapolis)

MISSISSIPPI
University of Mississippi

MISSOURI
University of Missouri, Columbia
> *University of Missouri, Columbia*

University of Missouri, Kansas City
> *University of Missouri, Kansas City*

Saint Louis University
> *Saint Louis University*

Washington University

NEBRASKA
Creighton University
University of Nebraska
> *University of Nebraska (not profiled)*

NEVADA
University of Nevada

NEW HAMPSHIRE
Dartmouth Medical School

NEW JERSEY
UMDNJ at Newark, NJ
College of New Jersey
Drew University
Montclair State University
New Jersey Institute of Technology
Richard Stockton College of New Jersey
Stevens Institute of Technology
UMDNJ/Robert Wood Johnson Medical School
Rutgers University

NEW MEXICO
University of New Mexico

NEW YORK
Albany Medical College
Rensselaer Polytechnic Institute
Union College
Sienna College
Albert Einstein College of Medicine of Yeshiva University
Columbia University
Cornell University Medical College
Mount Sinai
City University of New York Medical College
Sophie Davis School of Biomedical Education (not profiled)
New York University
New York University
University of Rochester
University of Rochester
SUNY Buffalo School of Medicine and Biomedical Sciences
University of Buffalo
SUNY Health Sciences Center at Brooklyn
Brooklyn College
SUNY Health Sciences Center at Syracuse
Binghamton University
SUNY Stony Brook Health Sciences Center
SUNY at StonyBrook

NORTH CAROLINA
Bowman Gray
Duke University
East Carolina University
University of North Carolina at Chapel Hill

NAGENDRA SAI KONERU, M.D.
VINEET ARORA, M.D.
OMAR WANG, ATC

NORTH DAKOTA
University of North Dakota

OHIO
Case Western Reserve University
Case Western Reserve University
University of Cincinnati
Medical College of Ohio
Northeastern Ohio Universities
University of Akron
Kent State University
Youngstown University
Ohio State University
Wright State University

OKLAHOMA
University of Oklahoma

OREGON
Oregon Health Sciences Center

PENNSYLVANIA
Jefferson Medical College of Thomas Jefferson University
Pennsylvania State University
MCP/Hanneman School of Medicine
Lehigh University
Villanova University
Hamot Medical Center and Medical College of Pennsylvania
Gannon University (Not profiled)
Pennsylvania State Medical College
University of Pennsylvania
University of Pittsburgh
Temple University

RHODE ISLAND
Brown University
Brown University

SOUTH CAROLINA
Medical University of South Carolina
University of South Carolina

THE HIGH SCHOOL DOCTOR
The Underground Roadmap to 6, 7, and 8 Year
Accelerated/Combined Medical Programs (BA/MD) in the United States

SOUTH DAKOTA
University of South Dakota

TENNESSEE
East Tennessee State University
East Tennessee State University
Meharry Medical College
Fisk University
University of Tennessee
Vanderbilt University

TEXAS
Baylor College of Medicine
Rice University
University of North Texas Health Sciences Center
Texas A&M University
University of Texas Health Sciences Center at San Antonio
Texas Tech Health Sciences Center
University of Texas at Dallas
University of Texas at Galveston
University of Texas at Houston

UTAH
University of Utah

VERMONT
University of Vermont

VIRGINIA
Eastern Virginia
The College of William and Mary
Hampton University
Norfolk State University
Old Dominion University
Virginia Commonwealth University
University of Virginia

WASHINGTON
University of Washington

WEST VIRGINIA
Marshall University
West Virginia University

NAGENDRA SAI KONERU, M.D.
VINEET ARORA, M.D.
OMAR WANG, ATC

WISCONSIN
Medical College of Wisconsin
University of Wisconsin at Madison
University of Wisconsin at Madison

THE HIGH SCHOOL DOCTOR
The Underground Roadmap to 6, 7, and 8 Year
Accelerated/Combined Medical Programs (BA/MD) in the United States

The Accelerated Medical Program Profiles

> *You must have control of the authorship of your own destiny. The pen that writes your life story must be held in your own hand.*
>
> *-Irene C. Kassorla*

There are nearly fifty accelerated (BA/MD) medical programs throughout the United States. Getting information on these programs was quite difficult and some programs were not very helpful. There were a few programs that were not included in our profiles due to the limited amount of information that was available to us. In addition, it is important to remember that application requirements are constantly changing, so don't conclude anything until you have received information directly from the programs. Through labor intensive research, we have provided you helpful profiles of each of the undergraduate components of the BA/MD programs. In addition we have given a star rating for several criteria which we felt were important:

1) **The undergraduate academic rating**: The undergraduate education that you will receive at the accelerated medical program is very important to consider. You must consider the possibility of perhaps not fulfilling the program requirements while in the program. What happens then? All you have to stand upon is the undergraduate school you chose. In addition, a good undergraduate education will make your medical school transition that much smoother. We looked at faculty to student ratio, student satisfaction, and faculty accessibility, as well as undergraduate reputation when we finalized our rating.

2) **Social atmosphere rating**: We have mentioned earlier not to underestimate the importance of your social experience while in school. It is important to have positive social outlets while in a stressful environment. Important elements such as location and extracurricular activities have been weighed in when deciding our rating.

3) **Tuition of the undergraduate campus**: Medical school is expensive enough! The expense of your undergraduate education will only compound your financial matters.
4) **Prestige of the associated medical school**: As mentioned earlier, the most definitive measurement of the quality of the BA/MD program lies in the quality of the associated medical school. Thus, we have rated the prestige of the associated medical school for each program.
5) **Overall score of the combined program**: We have given you a final score out of 100 so that you can have a measurable number to compare all of the programs.

All of the ratings are based on a 5 star scale or 5 dollar scale:
***** Superior
**** Excellent
*** Good
** Fair
* Poor

$$$$$: 25,000 +
$$$$: 20,000 – 25,000
$$$: 15,000-20,000
$$: 10,000-15,000
$: 5,000-10,000

**Binghamton University –
SUNY Health Sciences Center at Syracuse**
Rural Primary Care Recruitment Programs
College of Medicine
State University of New York
Health Science Center at Syracuse
P.O. Box 1000
Binghamton, NY 13902
(607)770-8618
davismatt@hscsyr.edu

State University of New York-Binghamton
Undergraduate Academic Rating: ***
Social Atmosphere Rating: ***
Tuition of the Undergraduate Campus: $
Prestige of the Associated Medical School:***
Overall Rating of the Combined Program: 82

PROGRAM TITLE:
BA/MD Program
8 year program

OPEN TO IN/OUT STATE STUDENTS:
Both in/out state students.

MINIMUM HIGH SCHOOL REQUIREMENTS:
GPA: 3.50
SAT: 1350
ACT: 30

MINIMUM UNDERGRADUATE REQUIREMENTS:
GPA: 3.30
MCAT: National Mean

APPLICATION DEADLINE:
December 15

SUNY-Binghamton University is a public institution located in Binghamton, New York, just above the Pennsylvania state lines. Last year, 42% of the approximately 16,500 applicants gained admittance. Many students who first set foot on the campus say they notice the beautiful landscape and buildings that surround the campus. They also notice the general education requirements that freshman or new students have to take. The program consists of an assortment of different concentration of classes. On average, the class size here is 28, while its student to faculty ratio is 19 to 1.

Similar to most state schools, introductory level courses are taught in a large lecture hall by the professor. However, these classes are broken down into smaller discussion groups facilitated by TA's. As far as ethnic diversity on campus, about 30% of the student population is from a minority background. With regards to campus resources, many students fell that they are well above par.

At SUNY-Binghamton, Greek life is quite popular. Around 16% of the student body belongs to either a fraternity or sorority. As far as the bar scene goes, most people hang out on State street. An alternative to the Greek life on campus and the bar scene, SUNY-Binghamton does offer over 150 groups and organizations a student can join ranging from photography to social service.

NAGENDRA SAI KONERU, M.D.
VINEET ARORA, M.D.
OMAR WANG, ATC

> **Boston University –**
> **Boston University School of Medicine**
> Associate Director, Admissions
> 121 Bay State Road
> Boston, MA 02215
> (617)353-2330
> admissions@bu.edu

Boston University
Undergraduate Academic Rating: ****
Social Atmosphere Rating: *****
Tuition of the Undergraduate Campus: $$$
Prestige of Associated Medical School: ****
Overall Rating of Combined Program: 90

PROGRAM TITLE:
BA/MD Program
7 year program

OPEN TO IN/OUT STATE STUDENTS:
Both in/out state students.

MINIMUM HIGH SCHOOL REQUIREMENTS:
GPA: 3.5
SAT: 1450
ACT: 33

MINIMUM UNDERGRADUATE REQUIREMENTS:
GPA: 3.0
MCAT: 28

APPLICATION DEADLINE:
December 15

Students usually love Boston, Massachusetts. Boston University receives about 28,000 applications per year, while it accepts about 50% of them. Boston University has a high academic rating because it has a decent faculty to student ration, professor accessibility rating, and the percentage of classes taught by TA's are pretty low. The average regular class size at BU is about 25 students. Boston University is a private university placed into an urban setting. The resources at Boston University are very good. The university offers over 130 majors. Students rate the campus as fairly unattractive; however, the city of Boston itself was noted to be great. If you are big on Greek life, Boston University may not be your top choice since Greek life is virtually non-existent compared to most state schools.

However, if you are into sports, Boston has plenty to offer. From the Boston Celtics to the Boston Red Sox, people from this town take their sports very seriously. With regards to sports on campus, the students attend NCAA sports quite frequently. Although varsity football has been let go by the athletic department, BU still fields a strong ice hockey team.

Boston is also known to be racially diverse city. One student said that Boston was the true melting pot of the United States. The University has over 100 countries that are represented. Some of the local hotspots outside of campus include Harvard Square, the famous fish market, and several pubs and breweries (including the one that the show "Cheers" was filmed at). The nightlife in Boston is very good. Boston has a potpourri of clubs, bars, and international restaurants according to one's tastes.

THE HIGH SCHOOL DOCTOR
The Underground Roadmap to 6, 7, and 8 Year
Accelerated/Combined Medical Programs (BA/MD) in the United States

Brandeis University – Tufts University School of Medicine
136 Harrison Avenue
Boston, Massachusetts 02111
(617) 636-6571
(Open only to Sophomores of Brandeis University)

Brandeis University
Undergraduate Academic Rating: ****
Social Atmosphere Rating: ***
Tuition of the Undergraduate Campus: $$$$
Prestige of Associated Medical School: ****
Overall Rating of Combined Program: 92

PROGRAM TITLE:
BA/MD Program
7 year program

OPEN TO IN/OUT STATE STUDENTS:
Both in/out state students.

MINIMUM HIGH SCHOOL REQUIREMENTS:
GPA: No minimum
SAT: No minimum
ACT: No Minimum

MINIMUM UNDERGRADUATE REQUIREMENTS:
GPA: 3.5
MCAT: National Mean

APPLICATION DEADLINE:
December 15

Brandeis University is a private institution located in Waltham, Massachusetts. Last year, over 5,700 high school students applied to Brandeis University with over half of the applicant pool gaining admittance. Similar to Tufts University, nearly all of the undergraduate classes are taught by the professors. The school also requires its students to finish their core curriculum program to gain a better-rounded education.

Brandeis University is also rated high for its research programs and its strong pre-professional programs. The average class size is 17, and the student to faculty ration is around 8 to 1. If you are looking to participate in intramural sports, this university offers very little in that regard. Greek life is also non-existent on campus because they don't have one.

> *"I felt that the strongest part of Brandeis were the amazing professors on campus. I was so impressed with my educational resources."*
> *- Josh Leiden, Senior*

In general, students find life at Waltham very uneventful because most of the student body is engrossed in the academic life for the majority of the day. Despite the volume of work that is placed on the students, many of them find solitude in the myriad of student organizations the school has to offer ranging from student government to yearbook. If you need a nightlife, Waltham is not the place to be on the weekends. Luckily for the students at Brandeis University, Boston is only five to ten minutes away.

NAGENDRA SAI KONERU, M.D.
VINEET ARORA, M.D.
OMAR WANG, ATC

> **Brooklyn College —**
> **SUNY Health Sciences Center at Brooklyn**
> **Director of Admissions**
> **Brooklyn College**
> **1602 James Hall**
> **Brooklyn, NY 11210**
> **(718)951-5044**

City University of New York-Brooklyn College
Undergraduate Campus Rating: **
Social Atmosphere Rating: ***
Tuition of the Undergraduate Campus: $
Prestige of the Associated Medical School: ***
Overall Rating of the Combined Program: 80

PROGRAM TITLE:
BA/MD Program
8 year program

OPEN TO IN/OUT STATE STUDENTS:
Both in/out state students.

MINIMUM HIGH SCHOOL REQUIREMENTS:
GPA: no minimum
SAT: no minimum
ACT: no minimum

MINIMUM UNDERGRADUATE REQUIREMENTS:
GPA: 3.50
MCAT: National Mean

APPLICATION DEADLINE:
December 15

CUNY-Brooklyn College is a public institution located in Brooklyn, New York. Brooklyn College has three academic divisions that offer up to 100 undergraduate majors on campus. Academically speaking, the average class size here is 35 while the student to faculty ratio is 14 to 1. For those who are looking for a social life on campus or would like to live on campus, unfortunately, all students who attend here commute to campus. In terms of ethnic diversity on campus, it is very similar to the environment of New York City. There is a plethora of minorities on campus. Around 45% of the undergraduate student body is African-American, Hispanic, or Asian American.

If you to have Greek life as part of your undergraduate experience, you may want to look elsewhere. Less than 2% of the student body is a member of the Greek System. However, Brooklyn College has over 120 different clubs and organizations a student can join. Students also enjoy participating in the intramural sports program. Although there are a lot of on campus events that happen on campus, many students who do not live in Brooklyn take advantage of living in New York City by going to beautiful sites such as the Brooklyn Museum and Botanical Garden, while other students go to Shea Stadium to catch a Mets baseball game via the subway system. For those looking for the nightlife, you have access to Manhattan. Locally, there are certainly enough clubs and bars to go to such as KLUB Europa of Brooklyn and Enigma Nightclub.

Brown University – Brown University School of Medicine
Program in Liberal Medical Education Office
Box G - A134
Providence, RI 02912
(401)863-2450

Brown University
Undergraduate Academic Rating: *****
Social Atmosphere Rating: **
Tuition of the Undergraduate Campus: $$$$
Prestige of Associated Medical School: *****
Overall Rating of Combined Program: 94

PROGRAM TITLE:
PLME Program
8 year program

OPEN TO IN/OUT STATE STUDENTS:
Both in/out state students.

MINIMUM HIGH SCHOOL REQUIREMENTS:
GPA: no minimum
SAT: no minimum; 1450 average
ACT: no minimum

MINIMUM UNDERGRADUATE REQUIREMENTS:
GPA: 3.0
MCAT: n/a

APPLICATION DEADLINE:
December 15

Unlike most universities, Brown University has a relaxed structured curriculum where there are no undergraduate course requirements. Thus, there are a wide variety of majors on can choose from. Brown University also carries a unique distinction of a having a grading system where a student can choose between two different grading systems where one option is a pass/no credit option while the other option is ABC/no credit.

Brown receives about 17,000 applications a year, however it only accepts about 15% of its applicants. Similar to other private universities, Brown has a small faculty to student ratio and a low percentage of classes that are taught by teacher assistants. Although getting into Brown is very competitive, once you are in, there is apparently no grade competition among the students.

> "I loved the education that I received at Brown University. The campus was so diverse and liberal. I would never trade my experience."
> -Swati Mothkar, Senior

Most of the nightlife occurs on-campus because there really isn't much to do in Providence. Although there are a lot of on campus activities, there is not much of a Greek life. Less than 15% of both men and women belong to either a fraternity or sorority. In terms of intercollegiate sports, many students do not attend many sporting events. Thus, there has been a question among a certain minority about the school's team spirit.

NAGENDRA SAI KONERU, M.D.
VINEET ARORA, M.D.
OMAR WANG, ATC

**Case Western Reserve University ---
Case Western Reserve University School of Medicine**
Office of Undergraduate Admission
10900 Euclid Avenue
Cleveland, OH 44106-7055
(216)368-4450
xx329@po.cwru.edu

Case Western University
Undergraduate Academic Rating: ****
Social Atmosphere Rating: ****
Tuition of the Undergraduate Campus: $$
Prestige of Associated Medical School: *****
Overall Rating of Combined Program: 93

PROGRAM TITLE:
Pre-professional Scholars Program (8 year program)

OPEN TO IN/OUT STATE STUDENTS:
Both in/out state students.

MINIMUM HIGH SCHOOL REQUIREMENTS:
GPA: No Minimum; 3.6 average
SAT: No minimum; 1410-1510 average
ACT: No Minimum; 28-33 average

MINIMUM UNDERGRADUATE REQUIREMENTS:
GPA: 3.3
MCAT: National Mean

APPLICATION DEADLINE:
December 15

CWRU is located in Cleveland, Ohio. It is a private school with less than 4,000 students. Despite the student to faculty ration is well below ten to one, students sometimes complain about the lack of personal attention they receive from the faculty. CWRU receives about 5,000 applications a year, but it accepts between 70 to 80% of them. In terms of Greek life, the men have eighteen national fraternities to choose from. On the other hand, the women have only four national sororities to choose from.

In terms of living in Cleveland, there are certainly a lot of things to do. Along with its diversity, the nightlife in Cleveland is incredible with the well-known "Flats" area. It is just a hotbed of bars and clubs in one small one to two mile area.

The resurgence of the NFL Browns a few years ago has certainly put Cleveland back on the map in terms of the professional sports scene. However, one of the many crown jewels of the city is Jacobs Field, one of the prettiest MLB baseball stadiums. Although the city has the Rock and Roll Hall of Fame and other historical parks and museums to go to, many students find it difficult to get around the campus and the city without a car.

THE HIGH SCHOOL DOCTOR
*The Underground Roadmap to 6, 7, and 8 Year
Accelerated/Combined Medical Programs (BA/MD) in the United States*

The College of New Jersey - UMDNJ - New Jersey Medical School
Office of Admissions
New Jersey Medical School
C-653 MSB
185 South Orange Avenue
Newark, NJ 07103-2714
(201) 982-4631

College of New Jersey
Undergraduate Academic Rating: ***
Social Atmosphere Rating: *
Tuition of the Undergraduate Campus: $
Prestige of Associated Medical School: ***
Overall Rating of Combined Program: 78

PROGRAM TITLE:
BA/MD Program
7 year program

OPEN TO IN/OUT STATE STUDENTS:
Both in/out state students.

MINIMUM HIGH SCHOOL REQUIREMENTS:
GPA: Top 10% of Class
SAT: 1400
ACT: 32

MINIMUM UNDERGRADUATE REQUIREMENTS:
GPA: 3.20
MCAT: National Mean

APPLICATION DEADLINE:
December 15

The College of New Jersey is a public institution located in Ewing, New Jersey. It is an hour train ride from both New York City and Philadelphia. Last year, over 6,300 students applied to the school with just under half of the applicants gaining admittance. For your money, the college of New Jersey is reasonably price for the quality of education you receive. Many students enjoy that, even though the school is a public institution, it has the feel and it acts much like a private one. The majority of the student body is mainly from New Jersey (95 Percent). As a result, many students from out of state feel left out in some social situations because the atmosphere can fell like one big high school. In terms of ethnic diversity, you can find it here, however, many ethnic groups tend to keep to themselves. In fact, there is not ethnic or racial integration.

On the academic side of the equation, the College of New Jersey has a student to faculty ratio of 12 to 1, and the average class size of a regular course is 23. One of the big pluses of the university is that the professors, not the teacher assistants, teach the freshman and sophomore classes. Students also rate the campus high on its looks and its computer and athletic facilities.

If you are looking for a great social life, don't' come here. Although there is a relatively strong Greek system, many students tend to go back home over the weekends because there is nothing to do in Ewing. Although there are around 150 student organizations and activities to choose from, many students feel that their peers don't get involved. Therefore, for most students who are seeking a night out on the town, they often go to Philadelphia or New York City.

NAGENDRA SAI KONERU, M.D.
VINEET ARORA, M.D.
OMAR WANG, ATC

The College of William and Mary — Eastern Virginia Medical School
Office of Admissions
Eastern Virginia Medical School
721 Fairfax Avenue
Norfolk, VA 23507-2000
(804)446-5812

The College of William and Mary
Undergraduate Academic Rating: ****
Social Atmosphere Rating: ***
Tuition of the Undergraduate Campus: $$
Prestige of the Associated Medical School: ***
Overall Rating of the Combined Program: 83

PROGRAM TITLE:
BA/MD Program
8 year program

OPEN TO IN/OUT STATE STUDENTS:
Both in/out state students.

MINIMUM HIGH SCHOOL REQUIREMENTS:
GPA: 3.50
SAT: 1350
ACT: 30

MINIMUM UNDERGRADUATE REQUIREMENTS:
GPA: 3.50
MCAT: National mean

APPLICATION DEADLINE:
December 15

The College of William and Mary is a public institution located in Williamsburg, Virginia. Last year, over 5,000 high students applied with about 40% of them gaining admittance to the university. The College of William and Mary is a beautiful campus I which a lot of history is shown in its architecture. The university's administration is also very traditional and historical in that it allows its students the right to take examinations unproctored. However, the courses at William and Mary are difficult and getting an A is well earned. The average class size at this university is around 26 while the student to faculty ratio is 12 to 1. Professors at William and Mary get mixed reviews. As far as the composition of the student body on campus, the majority of students are mainly white (86 Percent), while 64% of the undergraduates are from Virginia.

The Greek System dominates the social scene surrounding William and Mary. Nearly 30% of the student body is a member of the sixteen national fraternities or twelve notional sororities on campus. Although Williamsburg is a nice place to live, it does not offer much of a nightlife. The nightlife is pretty much the fraternities on campus. If the Greek life is not your style, there are over 300 student groups on campus to join. Other off campus options include going to Busch Gardens or hanging out at the Colonial National Historical Park. Plus, Virginia Beach is only about 40 minutes away.

Drew University
UMDNJ - New Jersey Medical School (MD)
Office of Admissions
New Jersey Medical School
C-653 MSB
185 South Orange Avenue
Newark, NJ 07103-2714
(201)982-4631

Drew University
Undergraduate Academic Rating: ****
Social Atmosphere Rating: *
Tuition of the Undergraduate Campus: $$$$
Prestige of Associated Medical School: ***
Overall Rating of Combined Program: 83

PROGRAM TITLE:
BA/MD Program
7 year program

OPEN TO IN/OUT STATE STUDENTS:
Both in/out state students.

MINIMUM HIGH SCHOOL REQUIREMENTS:
GPA: Top 10% of Class
SAT: 1400
ACT: n/a

MINIMUM UNDERGRADUATE REQUIREMENTS:
GPA: 3.40
MCAT: No minimum

APPLICATION DEADLINE:
January 7

Drew University is a private institution located in Madison, New Jersey. It is a train ride or twenty minute drive with no traffic to New York City. Last year, out of the 2,400 high school students that applied to Drew University, 1,800 of them gained admittance to the university. At Drew University, one of the things that struck us was the fact that every full-time freshman student receives a lab-top computer along with supporting software. After they graduate, it is theirs to keep.

I am sure that Drew University can afford to give computers away due to its high price tag for admission each year. However, even though Drew University tuition comes with a heavy cost, many students feel that the education they receive is worth the money. The average class size of a regular course is less than 20, and the professor teach all of the courses on campus. In fact, the student to faculty ratio is 12 to 1. Students also rate the athletic and computer facilities high in quality as well.

In terms of social life on campus, there is no Greek system. This is part of the reason why many students find the campus to be quiet and often boring during the weekend. Although Drew University is not known for its intercollegiate athletics, many members of the student body participate in intramural sports. Unfortunately, since it is a small institution, the school only offers just over sixty on campus organizations or activities to join. Like the college of New Jersey, most people tend to find their fun in New York City.

**Drexel University —
MCP Hahnemann University School of Medicine**
Office of Admissions
3141 Chestnut St.
Philadelphia, PA 19104
(800) 2-drexel
(215)895-2400

Drexel University
Undergraduate Academic Rating: ****
Social Atmosphere Rating: *****
Tuition of the Undergraduate Campus: $$
Prestige of Associated Medical School: ****
Overall Rating of Combined Program: 85

PROGRAM TITLE:
BA/MD Program
8 year program

OPEN TO IN/OUT STATE STUDENTS:
Both in/out state students.

MINIMUM HIGH SCHOOL REQUIREMENTS:
GPA: None; Top 10% of class
SAT: 1360
ACT: n/a

MINIMUM UNDERGRADUATE REQUIREMENTS:
GPA: 3.45
MCAT: Must Score the National Mean

APPLICATION DEADLINE:
January 15

Drexel University is a private institution located in the heart of Philadelphia, Pennsylvania. Last year, about 78% of the applicants who applied to Drexel University gained admittance. Right away, the first thing that many students enjoy about Drexel University is its location and the beauty of the campus. As a result, the resources of the university are good as well. However, many students also have noted that the professors place a lot of demands on its students academically. A lot of students though attend this university because of its cooperative education. This program allows and provides students with job experience in their choice of field before they graduate. And yes, these students get paid while working. At Drexel, the student to faculty ratio is 16 to 1, while the average class size here is 37. In terms of student body composition, minorities make up 25% of all undergraduates.

As for as the Greek life on campus, it is not that big here. Less than 7% of all undergraduates are Greek. Plus, many students study over the weekend. However, there are 103 groups and organizations for students to get involved outside of the classroom, and there are intramural sports being played regularly by both male and female students. In terms of the nightlife, many students use public transportation to head to downtown Philadelphia. During the day, many students flock over to the Philadelphia Art Museum. The Philadelphia Art Museum is well known not only for the art they have on display, it is also the place where the Rocky movie series was filmed.

East Tennessee State University – East Tennessee State University School of Medicine
Director, Premedical - Medical Program
Office of Medical Professions Advisement
P.O. Box 70,592
Johnson City, TN 37614-0592
(615)929-5602

East Tennessee State University
Undergraduate Academic Rating: **
Social Atmosphere Rating: **
Tuition of the Undergraduate Campus: $
Prestige of Associated Medical School: ***
Overall Rating of Combined Program: 73

PROGRAM TITLE:
BA/MD Program
8 year program

OPEN TO IN/OUT STATE STUDENTS:
Both in/out state students.

MINIMUM HIGH SCHOOL REQUIREMENTS:
GPA: Top 20% of class
SAT: 1190
ACT: 26

MINIMUM UNDERGRADUATE REQUIREMENTS:
GPA: 3.30
MCAT: National mean

APPLICATION DEADLINE:
December 15

East Tennessee State University is a public institution located in Johnson City, Tennessee. It is 90 miles northeast of Knoxville. ETSU has seven colleges offering over 100 academic programs. Last year, 79 percent of the approximately 3,000 applicants gained admittance. The library facilities should be good at ETSU considering that they pumped in $28 million dollars for new library that opened up two years ago.

The students rated the athletic and other academic facilities high. Academically speaking, the student to faculty ratio is 19 to 1. As for as the ethnic diversity on campus, minorities make up less than 10 percent of the student population. However, there are minority organizations are campus like the Chinese Scholar and Students Association or the Black Affairs Association

In terms of Greek life on campus, less than ten percent of the student body is a member of either a fraternity or sorority. However, many students are active in the other 215 student groups and organizations on campus. Students also participate in the popular intramural sports program at ETSU. There is actually an intramural handbook written and given to each sports team. As for as the nightlife in Johnson City, Bailey's Sports Grille should be checked out.

NAGENDRA SAI KONERU, M.D.
VINEET ARORA, M.D.
OMAR WANG, ATC

> **Fisk University –
> Meharry Medical College**
> Associate Vice President for College Relations and Lifelong Learning
> 1005 D.B. Todd, Jr. Boulevard
> Nashville, TN 37208
> (615)327-6425

Fisk University
Undergraduate Academic Rating: **
Social Atmosphere Rating: **
Tuition of the Undergraduate Campus: $
Prestige of the Associated Medical School: **
Overall Rating of the Combined Program: 72

PROGRAM TITLE:
BA/MD Program
7 year program

OPEN TO IN/OUT STATE STUDENTS:
Both in/out state students.

MINIMUM HIGH SCHOOL REQUIREMENTS:
GPA: 3.5
SAT: no minimum
ACT: no minimum

MINIMUM UNDERGRADUATE REQUIREMENTS:
GPA: 3.50
MCAT: National Mean

APPLICATION DEADLINE:
December 15

Fisk University is a private institution located in Nashville, Tennessee. It is a predominately African-American university. Last year, just over 800 applicants applied here with over 93% of the applicants gaining admittance. Fisk University is home to W.E.B. Dubois' alma mater. Due to its small enrollment, many students have a great relationship with the professors on campus.

Although some of the students complain that the professors place a lot of expectations on them, they are well respected by the student body. In a introductory level course, the average class size is 30, while the student to faculty ratio is 12 to 1. Due to its small size, the number of majors that are offered are limited. Students also note that the academic and athletic facilities need to be upgraded.

In terms of extracurricular activities on campus, there are a limited number of student organizations to join. However, there is a strong Greek system on campus where over 20% of the student population is either in a fraternity or sorority. Other than a move or hanging out on campus, most of the student body got to Greek parties. On occasion, many students go to downtown Nashville to get more of a nightlife. However, public transportation to and from Nashville can be difficult to arrange.

George Washington University –
George Washington University School of Medicine
Office of Admissions
George Washington University
2121 "I" Street, N.W.
Washington, DC 20052
(800)447-3765

George Washington University
Undergraduate Academic Rating: ****
Social Atmosphere Rating: *****
Tuition of the Undergraduate Campus: $$$$
Prestige of Associated Medical School: ****
Overall Rating of Combined Program: 90

PROGRAM TITLE:
BA/MD Program
7 year program

OPEN TO IN/OUT STATE STUDENTS:
Both in/out state students.

MINIMUM HIGH SCHOOL REQUIREMENTS:
GPA: 3.5
SAT: 1400
ACT: n/a

MINIMUM UNDERGRADUATE REQUIREMENTS:
GPA: 3.3
MCAT: Not Needed

APPLICATION DEADLINE:
December 15

George Washington University is a private institution located in Washington, DC. Last year, about half of the approximately 15,000 applicants gained admittance to the school. As one can imagine, there is a strong international flavor to this university with over 100 countries being represented. From the academic standpoint, many students find it nice that the professors teach most of the classes they take. In fact, TA's teaches only 3% of all the classes offered at GW and the student to faculty ratio is 12 to 1.

Unfortunately, like the U.S. Government, many students complain about the bureaucracy that is associated with the school such as registering for classes. At GW, you will find that the Greek life to be pervasive on campus with about 12% of the student body being a member of the Greek System. However, if you like to play sports, many students find that participation in intramural sports are pretty poor.

Like most big cities, GW offers a wonderful horde of stuff to do. From its historical monuments such as Capitol Hill to its public parks in West Potomac, you can't find a better location to stimulate your intellect. On the flip side, the nightlife in DC is exceptional. The Georgetown area is packed with European dance clubs, bars, and brewery pubs that are accessible via a car or a taxi. However, if you drive, parking is at a premium to this area, day or night.

NAGENDRA SAI KONERU, M.D.
VINEET ARORA, M.D.
OMAR WANG, ATC

> **Hampton University —
> Eastern Virginia Medical School**
> Office of Admissions
> Eastern Virginia Medical School
> 721 Fairfax Avenue
> Norfolk, VA 23507-2000
> (804)446-5812

Hampton University
Undergraduate Academic Rating: **
Social Atmosphere Rating: *
Tuition of the Undergraduate Campus: $
Prestige of the Associated Medical School: ***
Overall Rating of the Program: 73

PROGRAM TITLE:
BA/MD Program
8 year program

OPEN TO IN/OUT STATE STUDENTS:
Both in/out state students.

MINIMUM HIGH SCHOOL REQUIREMENTS:
GPA: 3.50
SAT: 1350
ACT: 30

MINIMUM UNDERGRADUATE REQUIREMENTS:
GPA: 3.50
MCAT: National mean

APPLICATION DEADLINE:
December 15

Hampton University is a private institution located in Hampton, Virginia. It is a historically an African-American school. Last year, 64% of the approximately 7,200 applicants gained admittance. Hampton University offers 47 undergraduate programs with Biology and Psychology being the preferred majors to study. Although it is a small institution, many of the students have difficulty in registering for their classes. The average class size at a regular course is 25 with the student to faculty ratio being 15 to 1. Many students at Hampton University find that the quality of education they receive is top-notch, however, there have to put in a lot of time toward their studies.

As far as on campus life is concerned, there is an enforced dress code and all freshman have to follow the 11:00PM curfew. In terms of a nightlife for the other students, many of them join the five national fraternities or four national sororities on campus. There are only 20 groups or organizations that are available to the student. Other than that, Hampton is a dead city to live in. As a result, many students attempt to take road trips to either Baltimore or Washington D.C.

Howard University – Howard University School of Medicine
Center for Preprofessional Education
P.O. Box 473
Administration Building
Washington, DC 20059
(202)806-7231

Howard University
Undergraduate academic rating: ****
Social Atmosphere rating: ****
Tuition of the Undergraduate Campus: $
Prestige of Associated Medical School: **
Overall Rating of Combined Program: 80

PROGRAM TITLE:
BA/MD Program
8 year Program

OPEN TO IN/OUT STATE STUDENTS:
Both in/out state students.

MINIMUM HIGH SCHOOL REQUIREMENTS:
GPA: 3.5
SAT: 1400
ACT: n/a

MINIMUM UNDERGRADUATE REQUIREMENTS:
GPA: 3.5
MCAT: Score the national mean

APPLICATION DEADLINE:
December 25

Howard University is a private institution located in Washington, DC. It is historically an African-American university. In fact, 98% of the student body is African-American. Last year, around 6,000 applications were made to Howard University with just over 50% of the applicant pool gaining admittance. The university itself is broken down to six school or departments offering a wide collection of subject areas and majors with African studies, music, and engineering being the strongest programs on record.

The average class size of the university is 18 and the student to faculty ratio is only 7 to 1. In terms of academic resources, Howard University provides great computer facilities in every residence hall and a great library. Many students also rate the faculty as top notch and very friendly. Perhaps the only negative is the fact that homework is very prevalent in the students' lives.

Unlike George Washington University, the student body is very active in intramural sports and very supportive of its intercollegiate sports program. In terms of Greek life, less than 5% of the student body is part of the Greek system, however, they do play a large role in the social climate and party scene of the university. In fact, despite the great off campus life that Washington DC has to offer, many students choose to stick around campus to hang out and socialize. However, many students at Howard University also note the easy access via public transportation to the MCI Center arena (home of the NHL's Washington Capitals and the NBA's Washington Wizards).

NAGENDRA SAI KONERU, M.D.
VINEET ARORA, M.D.
OMAR WANG, ATC

> **Illinois Institute of Technology —
> Chicago Medical School**
> Director of Admissions
> B.S./M.D. Program
> Illinois Institute of Technology
> 10 West 33rd Street
> Chicago, IL 60616
> 1-800-448-2329

Illinois Institute of Technology
University Academic Rating: **
Social Atmosphere Rating: ***
Tuition of the Undergraduate Campus: $$
Prestige of Associated Medical School: ***
Overall Rating of Combined Program: 80

PROGRAM TITLE:
BA/MD Program
8 year program

OPEN TO IN/OUT STATE STUDENTS:
Both in/out state students.

MINIMUM HIGH SCHOOL REQUIREMENTS:
GPA: 3.50
SAT: 1350
ACT: 30

MINIMUM UNDERGRADUATE REQUIREMENTS:
GPA: 3.50
MCAT: National Mean

APPLICATION DEADLINE:
December 15

Illinois Institute of Technology is a private school located in Chicago, Illinois. The university receives about 3,000 applications per year while it accepts about 65% of them. Although IIT has a good academic reputation, it is also known to place a lot of academic demands on its students.

The average class size is a whopping five. However, even though there is a decent Greek life at IIT, that is pretty much all there is to do on campus. If you plan to be active in sports after high school, don't look here either. IIT does not offer much of an intramural sports program. Also, the men to women ratio are close to three to one.

Although many students say the campus is not that attractive, they all currently enjoy their experience in Chicago and the diversity it offers, not only in culture, but also in things to do. With public transportation such as the "EL", the downtown area is just minutes away. So, if you are a sports fan, there are plenty of professional sporting events to go to such as watching a baseball game in Wrigley Field on a warm, sunny afternoon and having a couple of beers. If you are into the arts and sciences, the Chicago Museum of Science and Industry is also within reasonable distance. In terms of nightlife, Chicago offers a great club and bar scene for every individual's particular taste. A popular area for young adults is in Lincoln Park.

THE HIGH SCHOOL DOC.
The Underground Roadmap to 6, 7, and 8 Year
Accelerated/Combined Medical Programs (BA/MD) in the United States

Kent State University —
Northeastern Ohio Universities College of Medicine
4209 State Route 44
P.O. Box 95
Rootstown, Ohio 44272
(330)-325-2511

Kent State University
Undergraduate Academic Rating: ***
Social Atmosphere Rating: **
Tuition of the Undergraduate Campus: $
Prestige of Associated Medical School: ***
Overall Rating of Combined Program: 79

PROGRAM TITLE:
BA/MD Program
6 year program

OPEN TO IN/OUT STATE STUDENTS:
Both in/out state students.

MINIMUM HIGH SCHOOL REQUIREMENTS:
GPA: No Minimum
SAT: No Minimum
ACT: No Minimum

MINIMUM UNDERGRADUATE REQUIREMENTS:
GPA: 3.25
MCAT: Must Score an 8 on each section

APPLICATION DEADLINE:
December 15

Kent State University is a public institution located in Kent, Ohio. Last year, about 92% of the approximately 9,200 applicants gained admittance. For those of you who are history buffs, KSU was the place where the Ohio National Guard killed four university students and injured nine other university students during a student demonstration against the Vietnam War on May 4, 1970. There is a memorial dedicated to those students on campus.

Anyway, at Kent University, there are over 200 undergraduate majors and minors that are offered. The average class size on campus is 26 while the student to faculty ratio is 23 to 1. The undergraduates who come to Kent State University are mostly white (85 Percent). Students here note the great athletic facilities such as the on campus golf course, a bowling alley, and lighted basketball courts. In terms of Greek life on campus, there are 20 fraternities and 11 sororities on campus even though less than seven percent of the student body is Greek.

However, famous Greek Alumni from Kent State University are Lou Holtz and Drew Carey. As far as other on campus activities to join in, KSU has over 230 groups or organizations. In terms of the nightlife in Kent, the Rusty Nail, Sully's Tavern, and Screwy Louies are the places to go.

Lehigh University — MCP/Hanneman School of Medicine
Office of Admissions
Lehigh University
27 Memorial Drive West
Bethlehem, PA 18105
(610)758-3100

Lehigh University
Undergraduate Academic Rating: *****
Social Atmosphere Rating: ***
Tuition of the Undergraduate Campus: $$$$
Prestige of the Associated Medical School: ****
Overall Rating of the Combined Program: 87

PROGRAM TITLE:
BA/MD Program
6year program

OPEN TO IN/OUT STATE STUDENTS:
Both in/out state students.

MINIMUM HIGH SCHOOL REQUIREMENTS:
GPA: Top 5% of Class
SAT: 1360
ACT: 31

MINIMUM UNDERGRADUATE REQUIREMENTS:
GPA: 3.45
MCAT: Must score 9 on each section

APPLICATION DEADLINE:
December 15

Lehigh University is a private institution located in the industrial city of Bethleham, Pennsylvania. Last year, over 9,000 high school seniors applied to the university, while about 46% of them gain admittance. In general, many new students say they that the campus is beautiful. They also enjoy going to the new Zoellner Arts Center. Students also rave about the computer and athletic facilities on campus. However, Lehigh is one of the toughest academic schools in the country. Students note that is very difficult to get A's in many of the courses. However, many of the professors at this university were rated high on availability and accessibility. In a regular course at Lehigh, the average size of a class is 29. The student to faculty ratio at Lehigh is 12 to 1. As far as the composition of the student body, the majority of the undergraduates came from the East Coast. However, some students admit that there is not a large contingent of minorities on campus.

Due to the fact that students work hard during the week, many of the Lehigh undergraduates say they tend to party hard over the weekends. However, lately, the administration has tried to crack down on the alcohol use or abuse on campus. At Lehigh, many students belong to the Greek system. About one-third of the undergraduates on campus are Greek. In fact, many students say that the fraternity parties pretty much are the nightlife on the weekends. However, there are also a number of sporting events on can go to ranging from football to women's lacrosse. As far as the city of Bethleham is concerned, there is not much to do. Although the town is close to Philadelphia and New York City, many students note that the public transportation system to these urban areas are difficult and inaccessible.

THE HIGH SCHOOL DOCTOR
The Underground Roadmap to 6, 7, and 8 Year
Accelerated/Combined Medical Programs (BA/MD) in the United States

Michigan State University-
Michigan State University School of Medicine
College of Human Medicine
Office of Admissions
A-239 Life Sciences
East Lansing, MI 48824
(517)353-9620

Michigan State University
Undergraduate Academic Rating: ***
Social Atmosphere Rating: ****
Tuition of the Undergraduate Campus: $
Prestige of Associated Medical School: ***
Overall Rating of Combined Program: 86

PROGRAM TITLE:
BA/MD Pogram
8 year program

OPEN TO IN/OUT STATE STUDENTS:
Both in/out state students.

MINIMUM HIGH SCHOOL REQUIREMENTS:
GPA: 3.6; Top 10% of class
SAT: 1280
ACT: 29

MINIMUM UNDERGRADUATE REQUIREMENTS:
GPA: 3.20
MCAT: Not Needed

APPLICATION DEADLINE:
Rolling Admission

MSU is a large state school located in East Lansing, Michigan. The school offers over 150 majors. However, similar to other large state schools, the student to faculty ratio is quite high. Therefore, teacher assistants teach many of the freshman and sophomore classes. However, if you like to watch television, there are some classes that are taught using this type of medium.

MSU is not that hard of a school to get into if you have good grades and a decent SAT or ACT score. If you are a resident of Michigan and have the following aforementioned credentials, your admittance is pretty much a lock. Surprisingly, Greek life on campus is not as prevalent as in other large state schools. Less than 10% of both men and women are Greek. In terms of diversity, the student body is mainly white.

As for East Lansing itself, well, it isn't Boston or New York City in style and ambiance. However, there is a bevy of local bars and clubs to go to within reasonable walking distance depending on your place of residence. In terms of school spirit, and support of its athletic programs, MSU has no rival (except for the University of Michigan). Certainly, with their well-know tail-gaiting parties for the Fall football games and its strong basketball and ice hockey programs respectively, there is an ideal place to go for a college sports fan. In fact, on October 6, 2001, an outdoor hockey game is scheduled between the University of Michigan and Michigan State University at Spartan Stadium, the schools' football stadium. If all goes well, it can possibly break the world record for the largest audience to witness a ice hockey game.

NAGENDRA SAI KONERU, M.D.
VINEET ARORA, M.D.
OMAR WANG, ATC

Montclair State University — UMDNJ - New Jersey Medical School
Office of Admissions
New Jersey Medical School
C-653 MSB
185 South Orange Avenue
Newark, NJ 07103-2714

Montclair State University
Undergraduate Academic Rating: ***
Social Atmosphere Rating: **
Tuition of the Undergraduate Campus: $
Prestige of Associated Medical School: ***
Overall Rating of Combined Program: 76

PROGRAM TITLE:
BA/MD Program
7 year program

OPEN TO IN/OUT STATE STUDENTS:
Both in/out state students.

MINIMUM HIGH SCHOOL REQUIREMENTS:
GPA: Top 10% of Class
SAT: n/a
ACT: n/a

MINIMUM UNDERGRADUATE REQUIREMENTS:
GPA: n/a
MCAT: n/a

APPLICATION DEADLINE:
December 15

Montclair State University is a public institution located in Montclair, New Jersey. It is fifteen miles west of New York City. Last year, about 50% of the applicant pool gained admittance to Montclair State University. At this university, the females out number the males nearly two to one. Although 96% of the undergraduate students are from New Jersey, about one-third of the student body is African-American, Hispanic, and Asian American. There are five undergraduate schools on campus where 44 undergraduate majors are offered with psychology and biology being the preferred majors for most of the undergraduate students. As for as the schools resources go, the athletic facilities receive most the praise from the students. Academically speaking, the student to faculty ratio here is 16 to 1.

In terms of Greek life on campus, many students here enjoy that aspect of life the university has to offer. There are 25 local and notional fraternities for the men and 17 local and national sororities for women. However, many students enjoy participating in the intramural sports program on campus. The sports offered range from flag football to inner-tube waterpolo. Students can also participate in the over 100 student groups or organizations. These organizations help sponsor and run popular events on campus like Spring Week. However, since New York City is close to the college, many students take advantage of their location and enjoy what the city has to offer them.

**New Jersey Institute of Technology -
UMDNJ - New Jersey Medical School**
Office of Admissions
New Jersey Medical School
C-653 MSB
185 South Orange Avenue
Newark, NJ 07103-2714
(201)982-4631

New Jersey Institute of Technology
Undergraduate Academic Rating: ****
Social Atmosphere Rating: **
Tuition of the Undergraduate Campus: $
Prestige of Associated Medical School: ***
Overall Rating of Combined Program: 81

PROGRAM TITLE:
BA/MD Program
7 year program

OPEN TO IN/OUT STATE STUDENTS:
Both in/out state students.

MINIMUM HIGH SCHOOL REQUIREMENTS:
GPA: Top 10% of Class
SAT: 1400
ACT: n/a

MINIMUM UNDERGRADUATE REQUIREMENTS:
GPA: 3.20
MCAT: National Mean

APPLICATION DEADLINE:
December 15

New Jersey Institute of Technology is a located in Newark, New Jersey. Newark is located right across from New York City. Last year, around 64% of the approximately 4,100 applicants gained admittance into this institution. At the NJIT, the academic strength of the university is in its Engineering program. Here, students feel that it is easy to get into NJIT, however, they quickly respond by saying that it is more difficult to remain enrolled at NJIT due to its high academic standards. Due to its intense curriculum and standards, many students do not have much of a social life. In terms of ethnic diversity, it is quite pervasive here on this campus. In fact, many students state that its ethnic diversity is one of the strengths of the school. However, the school is also known for its lack of women attending the school.

From the academic standpoint, NJIT's average class size is 25, with its student to faculty ratio being 13 to 1. Like Drew University, all freshmen that are registered as full time students receive a computer and supporting software packages. Despite the small class size, many students complain about not being able to understand some of their professors due to their heavy international accents they do carry.

As mentioned earlier, the social life is not top sirloin quality. However, many students do drink over the weekends to compliment the long hours of studying that they do. Although they do offer some on campus activities, many of them choose not to participate in them. Many students at NJIT look to New York City as an alternative form of entertainment.

NAGENDRA SAI KONERU, M.D.
VINEET ARORA, M.D.
OMAR WANG, ATC

> **New York University ---
> New York University School of Medicine**
> Admissions Office
> College of Arts & Science
> 22 Washington Square North
> Room 904 Main Building
> New York, NY 10003
> (212)998-4500
> admissions@nyu.edu

New York University
Undergraduate Academic Rating: *****
Social Atmosphere Rating: *****
Tuition of the Undergraduate Campus: $$$$
Prestige of Associated Medical School: *****
Overall Rating of Combined Program: 96

PROGRAM TITLE:
BA/MD Program
8 year program

OPEN TO IN/OUT STATE STUDENTS:
Both in/out state students.

MINIMUM HIGH SCHOOL REQUIREMENTS:
GPA: 3.8
SAT: 1450
ACT: n/a

MINIMUM UNDERGRADUATE REQUIREMENTS:
GPA: n/a
MCAT: National Mean

APPLICATION DEADLINE:
January 15

NYU is a private institution located in the heart of New York City. More specifically, NYU is in the center of Washington Square Park. Due to its location and academic reputation, nearly 29,000 applicants applied to NYU with only about one third of them gaining admittance. Academically and faculty wise, NYU is, no question, one of the top universities in the country. The professors are knowledgeable, and the number of academic programs NYU has to offer is unparalleled. The average class size in a typical NYU course is below 30 while its student to faculty ratio is 13 to 1. Like the city, ethnic diversity is very customary at NYU. However, one of the drawbacks of NYU is the lack of on campus housing for its full time students. However, recently, there has been some positive movement to rectify this situation.

With regard to the social life in New York City, there is plenty of stuff to do on campus as well as off campus. There are over 250 student groups that one can get involved with. In terms of Greek life, NYU has eleven national fraternities and seven national sororities. However, not many students are active in intramural sports nor do they support their intercollegiate sports on campus. Consequently, school spirit here is not as pervasive compared to other collegiate institutions.

As mentioned earlier in this book, location of your school is probably on the main factors that you should consider when you apply to these accelerated medical school programs. As a result, if you value a nightlife/club life or enjoy sampling a wide variety of different cultures and tastes, NYU should be one of your top choices. One of the great aspects of New York City and the university is the fact that the subway system is incredible. Consequently, access to midtown or Chinatown is easy via subway from NYU. What is the cost to you? Only a $1.50 each way.

NAGENDRA SAI KONERU, M.D.
VINEET ARORA, M.D.
OMAR WANG, ATC

> **Norfolk State University —
> Eastern Virginia Medical School**
> Office of Admissions
> Eastern Virginia Medical School
> 721 Fairfax Avenue
> Norfolk, VA 23507-2000
> (804)446-5812

Norfolk State University
Undergraduate Academic Rating: ***
Social Atmosphere Rating: ***
Tuition of the Undergraduate Campus: $
Prestige of the Associated Medical School: ***
Overall Rating of the Combined Program: 81

PROGRAM TITLE:
BA/MD Program
8 year program

OPEN TO IN/OUT STATE STUDENTS:
Both in/out state students.

MINIMUM HIGH SCHOOL REQUIREMENTS:
GPA: 3.50
SAT: 1350
ACT: 30

MINIMUM UNDERGRADUATE REQUIREMENTS:
GPA: 3.50
MCAT: National Mean

APPLICATION DEADLINE:
December 15

Norfolk State University is a public institution located in Norfolk, Virginia. Last year, 82% of the high school seniors who applied gained admittance. NSU is one of the largest African-American universities in the country. At NSU, there are five undergraduate schools or divisions that offer 37 undergraduate academic programs. Academically speaking, the student to faculty ratio is 22 to 1. Students are NSU note that facilities on campus are adequate for them. One of the nice things about this school is that it has this program called "NSU Cluster" where it creates opportunities for its students to intern and perhaps eventually work with business in the Norfolk community. There are 10 fraternities and sororities on campus and 80 student organizations that a NSU student can join. Campus activities range from gospel choir to pep club.

In general, many of the students are very supportive of the "Spartans" on campus. Norfolk State University is part of the MEAC Conference. NSU has the third largest football stadium in Division I-AA football, and usually all of the 30,000 seats are taken by the student body or by the local community. Even though most students following the intercollegiate sports, most students spend their free time going to the public beaches and bike trails in Norfolk.

> **Northwestern University –
> Northwestern University School of Medicine**
> Office of Admission and Financial Aid
> 1801 Hinman Avenue
> Evanston, IL 60204-3060
> (708)491-7271
> ug-admission@nwu.edu

Northwestern University
Undergraduate Academic Rating: *****
Social Atmosphere Rating: *****
Tuition of the Undergraduate Campus: $$$$$
Prestige of Associated Medical School: *****
Overall Rating of Combined Program: 96

PROGRAM TITLE:
HPME
7 year program

OPEN TO IN/OUT STATE STUDENTS:
Both in/out state students.

MINIMUM HIGH SCHOOL REQUIREMENTS:
GPA: No minimum
SAT: No minimum
ACT: No minimum

MINIMUM UNDERGRADUATE REQUIREMENTS:
GPA: 2.75 overall; 3.00 in science classes
MCAT: Not needed

APPLICATION DEADLINE:
December 15

Northwestern University is a private institution located in Evanston, Illinois. Evanston is located just north of the city of Chicago. Out of the schools we have listed in this book, Northwestern is one of the toughest schools to get into. Last year, only one out of every three applicants gained admittance into Northwestern. Academically, like most Ivy League schools, Northwestern is noted for its tough academic standards where every one of the students on campus has to earn their grade through hard work.

Unlike most schools that have semester sessions, Northwestern goes by the quarter system that could make life for those procrastinators a little bit harder. In general, the majority of the classes are small and the professors will give you the time of day to answer any questions, comments or concerns you may have. Like most top-tier schools, Northwestern offers a bevy of academic majors with engineering and journalism being noted as the most popular among the undergraduate students.

Unlike UIC, Northwestern has a strong Greek system. About 30% of the undergraduate student body is a member of the Greek system. For those who want something different than the Greek life, there are on campus activities like intramural sports or other academic organizations.

In terms of the social scene in Evanston, there is not much there other than fraternity parties. If you need to get away from campus, most students take the "EL" and go downtown to Chicago where different and unique opportunities exist. For those into college sports, Northwestern is in the Big Ten Conference. Even though it is a small school, the majority of the student body tailgates on football Saturdays and cheer on their Wildcats just like any other big university.

NAGENDRA SAI KONERU, M.D.
VINEET ARORA, M.D.
OMAR WANG, ATC

Old Dominion University — Eastern Virginia Medical School
Office of Admissions
Eastern Virginia Medical School
721 Fairfax Avenue
Norfolk, VA 23507-2000
(804)446-5812

Old Dominion University
Undergraduate Academic Rating: ****
Social Atmosphere Rating: **
Tuition of the Undergraduate Campus: $$
Prestige of Associated Medical School: ***
Overall Rating of the Program: 80

PROGRAM TITLE:
BA/MD Program
8 year program

OPEN TO IN/OUT STATE STUDENTS:
Both in/out state students.

MINIMUM HIGH SCHOOL REQUIREMENTS:
GPA: 3.50
SAT: 1350
ACT: 30

MINIMUM UNDERGRADUATE REQUIREMENTS:
GPA: 3.50
MCAT: National mean

APPLICATION DEADLINE:
December 15

ODU is a public institution located in Norfolk, Virginia. Last year, 70% of the high school seniors who applied gained admittance to ODU. There are approximately 13,000 undergraduate students at ODU with over 100 countries being represented. In fact, minorities represent one-third of the undergraduate student body.

At ODU, sixty-four bachelor degree programs are offered amongst its six academic colleges. Academically speaking, the average class size here is around 23, while the student to faculty ratio is 15 to 1. As far as resources go, its students rated both the athletic and academic facilities high. On campus, the computer facilities are accessible twenty-four hours a day.

At this university, less than 10% of the undergraduate student population is a member of the Greek system. Although the Greek system is not actively involved by the students, many of the students involve themselves with the over student organizations or groups on campus. The university also holds great annual events such as the Every Women's Festival and Unity Week. As for as support for its intercollegiate athletics, there is wonderful support from the student body for its women's basketball, women's soccer, and women's field hockey teams. As for as the nightlife goes, if you have a car, many students choose to go to Busch Gardens in Williamsburg or go to Virginia Beach to enjoy the sun during the spring and summer months.

THE HIGH SCHOOL DOCTOR
*The Underground Roadmap to 6, 7, and 8 Year
Accelerated/Combined Medical Programs (BA/MD) in the United States*

> **Pennsylvania State University —
> Thomas Jefferson Medical College**
> Undergraduate Admissions
> Pennsylvania State University
> 201 Shields Building - Box 3000
> University Park, PA 16802
> (814)865-5471

Pennsylvania State University
Undergraduate Academic Rating: ****
Social Atmosphere Rating: *****
Tuition of the Undergraduate Campus: $$
Prestige of Associated Medical School: ****
Overall Rating of Combined Program: 90

PROGRAM TITLE:
Pre-medical Program
6 year program

OPEN TO IN/OUT STATE STUDENTS:
Both in/out state students.

MINIMUM HIGH SCHOOL REQUIREMENTS:
GPA: None; Top 10% of Class
SAT: 1440
ACT: n/a

MINIMUM UNDERGRADUATE REQUIREMENTS:
GPA: 3.20
MCAT: National Mean

APPLICATION DEADLINE:
December 1

Penn State University is a public institution located in University Park, Pennsylvania. Last year, over 28,000 high school seniors applied to PSU with about half of them getting in. PSU is one of the largest public institutions in the country. Its total undergraduate enrollment last year was approximately 34,000. With a big school, you get great academic resources on campus. PSU also offers a plethora of majors to choose from. However, because of its large size, it is difficult to get personalized attention as far as your academics are concerned. Lecture class sizes for introductory courses are in the hundreds, and TA's teaches the majority of the upper-tier courses. The average class size at PSU is 26, while the student to faculty ratio is 19 to 1. Students also point out that registration can be difficulty on campus as well. Certainly, at PSU, you have to be proactive regarding your education. As for as ethnic diversity on campus, it is prevalent on campus. However, since the campus is so big, it is difficult to notice it.

Although there may be certain academic disadvantages at PSU, the social life is incredible. For starters, the Greek system is very popular in Happy Valley. About 15% of the total student body belongs to either a fraternity or sorority. There is also strong support from the student body with regards to its intercollegiate athletic program. No question that football and Coach Joe Paterno is king at PSU despite having a lousy year in 2000, however, other sports such as wrestling, women's volleyball, and women's basketball have also gained a share of the national spotlight. Due to the fact that life on campus seems to revolve on sports, many students actively participants in the 29 intramural sports the university offers.

Despite the strong athletic presence and party atmosphere on campus, there are other alternative forms of entertainment. PSU offers around 400 groups and

NAGENDRA SAI KONERU, M.D.
VINEET ARORA, M.D.
OMAR WANG, ATC

organizations for students to join. Students can also socialize at the HUB, the on campus student union. Off campus, for those who are more outdoorsy, hiking trails, lakes, and ski slopes surrounds PSU.

Rensselaer Polytechnic Institute — Albany Medical College
47 New Scotland Avenue
Albany, New York 12208
(518) 262-5521

Rensselaer Polytechnic Institute
Undergraduate Academic Rating: ***
Social Atmosphere Rating: **
Tuition of the Undergraduate Campus: $$$$
Prestige of Associated Medical School: ***
Overall Rating of Combined Program: 81

PROGRAM TITLE:
BA/MD Program
7 Year Program

OPEN TO IN/OUT STATE STUDENTS:
Both in/out state students.

MINIMUM HIGH SCHOOL REQUIREMENTS:
GPA: no minimum
SAT: no minimum
ACT: no minimum

MINIMUM UNDERGRADUATE REQUIREMENTS:
GPA: 3.20
MCAT: Not needed

APPLICATION DEADLINE:
December 1

RPI is a private institution located in Troy, New Jersey. It is about three to four hours away from the major cities such as Boston, New York, and Montreal. Last year, about 73% of the approximately 5,500 high school students who applied gained admittance to the university. RPI is mostly an engineering school where the majority of its students studying a lot during the week. The average class size at RPI is 19 while its student to faculty ratio is 13 to 1. Students at RPI rate the professors being very professional, but not very personable. RPI offers great ethnic diversity to its students, however the male to female ratio is close to three to one. Consequently, the majority of the male students go to nearby state schools looking to meet members of the opposite sex.

Two things dominate the social life at RPI: (1) The RPI Ice Hockey team and (2) the Greek system. Although RPI is a Division III university, the men's ice hockey team is Division I. As far as the Greek system goes, 8% of the student body is a member of the Greek system. However, the fraternity houses host the majority of the on campus party scene. In fact, some students feel that the fraternity parties are the only game in town. As far as the weather goes, it is not Miami or Los Angeles. Many students wish it were better.

The RPI accelerated medical program is focused on research, while the one in Union College is focused on health management and the one in Siena College is focused on community service, all three of which are associated with Albany Medical College

NAGENDRA SAI KONERU, M.D.
VINEET ARORA, M.D.
OMAR WANG, ATC

**Rice University –
Baylor College of Medicine**
Office of Admissions
One Baylor Plaza
Room 106A
Houston, TX 77030
(713)798-4841

Rice University
Undergraduate Academic Rating: *****
Social Atmosphere Rating: *****
Tuition of the Undergraduate Campus: $$
Prestige of the Associated Medical School: *****
Overall Rating of the Combined Program: 97

PROGRAM TITLE:
BA/MD Program
8 year program

OPEN TO IN/OUT STATE STUDENTS:
Both in/out state students.

MINIMUM HIGH SCHOOL REQUIREMENTS:
GPA: No minimum
SAT: No minimum
ACT: No minimum

MINIMUM UNDERGRADUATE REQUIREMENTS:
GPA: 3.20
MCAT: Not needed

APPLICATION DEADLINE:
December 15

Rice University is a private institution located in the heart of Houston, Texas. Last year, around 6,800 applicants applied here with only 23% of the total applicant pool gaining admittance. Rice is one of the smallest universities on our list. However, it has the lowest student to faculty ratio of 5 to 1. On average, the class size for a regular course is 18. Rice is also one the cheaper private schools in the country. Although students have the luxury of taking any class they desire, students say that the academic standards are set pretty high. However, many students, unlike other institutions, don't feel that there is a lot of bureaucratic red tape surrounding the campus administration.

As far as extracurricular activities go on campus, Rice does not have a Greek system. However, there are over 200 student groups on can get involved with. Also, there are a number of popular events on campus ranging from the "Annual Beer-Bike Race" to the Night of Decadence. There are also 12 intramural sports for both men and women to participate in. Most students also support the 14 intercollegiate sports on campus. In terms of the student body composition, only 45% of the undergraduates are from Texas. As a result, there is a great mix of different people from different backgrounds that are exhibited at Rice University. In fact, one-third of the undergraduate student population is either African-American, Hispanic, or Asian American.

THE HIGH SCHOOL DOCTOR
The Underground Roadmap to 6, 7, and 8 Year
Accelerated/Combined Medical Programs (BA/MD) in the United States

Richard Stockton College of New Jersey - UMDNJ - New Jersey Medical School
Office of Admissions
New Jersey Medical School
C-653 MSB
185 South Orange Avenue
Newark, NJ 07103-2714
(201)982-4631

Richard Stockton College of New Jersey
Undergraduate Academic Rating: ***
Social Atmosphere Rating: ****
Tuition of the Undergraduate Campus: $
Prestige of Associated Medical School: ***
Overall Rating of Combined Program: 82

PROGRAM TITLE:
BA/MD Program
7 year program

OPEN TO IN/OUT STATE STUDENTS:
Both in/out state students.

MINIMUM HIGH SCHOOL REQUIREMENTS:
GPA: Top 10% of Class
SAT: 1400
ACT: n/a

MINIMUM UNDERGRADUATE REQUIREMENTS:
GPA: 3.20
MCAT: National Mean

APPLICATION DEADLINE:
December 15

Richard Stockton College of New Jersey is a public institution located in Pomona, New Jersey. Atlantic City is about a 20-minute drive from the campus and about a 50-minute drive to Philadelphia with no traffic. Last year, over 3,000 applicants applied to this institution with less than half of them making the cut. At this college, 97% of the students are from New Jersey. The average class size here is 17, while the student to faculty ratio is 25 to 1. The college offers 39 undergraduate majors. As far as diversity on campus, there several minority organizations one can join ranging from the Unified Black Student's society to the Asian Student Alliance.

If you are looking for a strong Greek presence on campus, you will be hard pressed to find it here. Only around 5% of the student population is Greek. There are 73 student-sponsored groups or organizations on campus. However, the intramural and intercollegiate sports here are pretty big. The intramural sports program even has its own website. The sports that this college carries are flag football, volleyball, basketball, soccer, street hockey, and softball. As for as living in Pomona, it is located right in between Atlantic City and Philadelphia. If you have access to a car, you can enjoy the nightlife in either city. In Atlantic City, of course, it is the Las Vegas of the East. There are plenty of places to gamble such as the Taj Majal and the Trump Plaza. You can also catch a minor league baseball game watching the Atlantic City Surf.

NAGENDRA SAI KONERU, M.D.
VINEET ARORA, M.D.
OMAR WANG, ATC

Rutgers University - UMDNJ - Robert Wood Johnson Medical School
Bachelor/Medical Degree Program
Nelson Biological Laboratory
Rutgers University
P.O. Box 1059
Piscataway, NJ 08855-1059
(908)445-5270

Rutgers University
Undergraduate Academic Rating: ***
Social Atmosphere Rating: ***
Tuition of the Undergraduate Campus: $
Prestige of Associated Medical School: ***
Overall Rating of Combined Program: 80

PROGRAM TITLE:
BA/MD Program
8 year program

OPEN TO IN/OUT STATE STUDENTS:
Both in/out state students.

MINIMUM HIGH SCHOOL REQUIREMENTS:
GPA: Top 10% of Class
SAT: 1200
ACT: n/a

MINIMUM UNDERGRADUATE REQUIREMENTS:
GPA: 3.30
MCAT: National Mean

APPLICATION DEADLINE:
December 15

Rutgers University is a public institution located in Piscataway, New Jersey. However, Rutgers University has university sites also in Newark, Camden, and New Brunswick respectively, where New Brunswick contains the largest concentration of the undergraduate student body. As you can see, it is a large state school in which it is broken up into eighteen undergraduate college divisions. Due to its growing reputation as a good state academic institution, over 20,000 high school students applied to Rutgers University with about half of them gaining admittance.

Rutgers offers nearly 100 majors with economics and biology being the most popular. In terms of the ethnic composition of the school, the ethnic diversity Rutgers has to offer is quite good. With regard to its academics, on average, the class size is 46, with about twenty-five percent of the classes being taught by TA's. Many of the students feel that if you want to get things done academically, the professors at Rutgers will offer little assistance in that regard.

"Rutgers is the most diverse campus I have ever seen. The only problem is that most minority groups have a tendency to stick together in their own little clique."
-Radhika Krishnamurthi, Sophomore

As far as activities go, Rutgers offers a wide range of social and political activities a student can engage in. If you are looking for a Greek life, only two percent of the student population is Greek.

Perhaps another disadvantage of the university's Greek system is the fact that all of the Greek housing is off campus. However, the majority of the nightlife occurs at the fraternity houses.

As far as living in New Brunswick, most university students say that it is not a bad place to go out on the town once in a while; however, there are areas that are questionable to pass through. However, in the spring and summer, some students take advantage of going to the Jersey Shore, which is a beach area along the coast of New Jersey, to get some sun. To get more of a nightlife, the majority of the students head to New York City or Philadelphia.

NAGENDRA SAI KONERU, M.D.
VINEET ARORA, M.D.
OMAR WANG, ATC

**St. Louis University –
St. Louis University Health Sciences Center**
Scholars Program in Medicine
1402 South Grand Boulevard
St. Louis, MO 63104
(314)-577-8205

Saint Louis University
Undergraduate Academic Rating: ***
Social Atmosphere Rating: ****
Tuition of the Undergraduate Campus: $$
Prestige of Associated Medical School: ***
Overall Rating of Combined Program: 81

PROGRAM TITLE:
BA/MD Program
7 year Program

OPEN TO IN/OUT STATE STUDENTS:
Both in/out state students.

MINIMUM HIGH SCHOOL REQUIREMENTS:
GPA: 3.6
SAT: n/a
ACT: 30

MINIMUM UNDERGRADUATE REQUIREMENTS:
GPA: 3.50
MCAT: Must Score the National Mean

APPLICATION DEADLINE:
December 15

SLU is a Roman Catholic School located in St. Louis, Missouri. One of the schools great strengths is their pre-professional programs and its faculty. Many students give their professor's a "thumbs-up" rating in terms of the quality of education that they are receiving. With regards to diversity, students rate their peers as very friendly and easy to get along with.

The average class size is about 17 students. Although the students feel the campus is fairly unattractive, they enjoy the fact that they live in St. Louis. In terms of admittance, about 70% of the 5,000 applicants are accepted. If you want to have a Greek life, SLU has a strong Greek life compared to other private universities.

Saint Louis itself is a great city.

There are a number of bars and clubs surrounding the campus and within the greater downtown area. Saint Louis also is one of the few cities that have gambling. Gambling places such as Harrah's are only 15 to 20 minutes away from campus. If that particular nightlife doesn't fit your profile, there are lot of parks and professional sporting events one can go to during the school year. Popular things include watching a Cardinals baseball game or a Rams football game.

THE HIGH SCHOOL DOCTOR
The Underground Roadmap to 6, 7, and 8 Year
Accelerated/Combined Medical Programs (BA/MD) in the United States

Siena College — Albany Medical College
47 New Scotland Avenue
Albany, New York 12208
(518) 262-5521

Siena College
Undergraduate Academic Rating: **
Social Atmosphere Rating: ***
Tuition of the Undergraduate Campus: $$
Prestige of Associated Medical School: ***
Overall Rating of Combined Program: 78

PROGRAM TITLE:
BA/MD Program
8 year program

OPEN TO IN/OUT STATE STUDENTS:
Both in/out state students.

MINIMUM HIGH SCHOOL REQUIREMENTS:
GPA: No minimum
SAT: No minimum
ACT: n/a

MINIMUM UNDERGRADUATE REQUIREMENTS:
GPA: 3.40
MCAT: Not needed

APPLICATION DEADLINE:
December 1

Siena College is a private Roman Catholic institution located in Loudonville, New York, just two miles north of Albany. Last year, two-thirds of the approximately 3,700 applicants gained admittance. At Siena College, one of the positives of the university is students have 24 hour access to all the computer facilities on campus. There are also no fees or time limits placed on the students. Students also note the wonderful athletic facilities they have as well. Academically, there are three undergraduate schools offering twenty-four majors. The average class size is around 22, while the student to faculty ratio is 14 to 1. Another bonus of the school is the fact that very few TA's teach introductory courses here. However, in terms of diversity, less than 10% of the student body is minorities.

If you are looking for a Greek life on campus, Siena College does not have a Greek System. However, they have around 70 groups or organizations that one can join ranging from the Accounting Club to the Yo-yo club. Many students on campus support the intercollegiate sports on campus with Men's Basketball and Football being the most popular. For the collegiate wrestling fans, the NCAA Division I 2002 Wrestling Championships will be held in Albany, New York at the Pepsi Center. Although there are a lot of sporting events to go to, students can also enjoy non-athletic activities during the year from school-sponsored events like Siena Fest and Siblings Weekend. On the weekends, the place to go is to Albany. The hotspots in Albany include Northern Lights, Big House Brewery Company, or Valentine's.

NAGENDRA SAI KONERU, M.D.
VINEET ARORA, M.D.
OMAR WANG, ATC

State University of New York at Stony Brook –
SUNY Stony Brook Health Sciences Center
Scholars In Medicine Program
Honors College
Stony Brook, New York 11794-3357
(631)632-4378

State University of New York at Stony Brook
Undergraduate Academic Rating: ****
Social Atmosphere Rating: ***
Tuition of the Undergraduate Campus: $
Prestige of Associated Medical School: ***
Overall Rating of Combined Program: 82

PROGRAM TITLE:
Scholars For Medicine Program
8 year Program

OPEN TO IN/OUT STATE STUDENTS:
Both in/out state students.

MINIMUM HIGH SCHOOL REQUIREMENTS:
GPA: No Minimum
SAT: 1350
ACT: n/a

MINIMUM UNDERGRADUATE REQUIREMENTS:
GPA: 3.40
MCAT: National Mean

APPLICATION DEADLINE:
December 15

SUNY-Stony Brook is a public institution located in Stony Brook, New York. More specifically, the school is on Long Island where New York City is 60 west of the university. Last year, about 15,000 high school students applied to SUNY-Stony Brook. Approximately 55% of them gained admittance to the university. Many students here enjoy the peaceful surroundings and beauty of the campus. Academically speaking, there are five undergraduate schools where there are over 50 majors to choose from. Although graduate students teach over 40% of the introductory courses, many students rate their professors high in accessibility as well as academically. On average, the regular course size is around 38, however, the student to faculty ratio is only 11 to 1. In terms of ethnic diversity, Asian Americans make up twenty-three percent of the undergraduate students on campus, while less than 10% of the student population is African-American.

In terms of social activities on campus, many students say that Stony Brook is sometimes boring over the weekends. Considering that ninety-five percent of the undergraduate student population is from New York, many of these students go home for the weekend. Although there is a Greek system on campus, they do not have fraternity or sorority housing on campus. However, many students join the 140 groups and organizations on campus. Many students also take advantage of the upgraded sports facilities on campus. These facilities include twenty tennis courts, two sand volleyball courts, and a 400-meter track. At SUNY-Stony Brook, there are 50 intramural sports for both men and women to participate in. If you want a good nightlife, you have to pack your bag and jump on the train from Stony Brook to Manhattan. It is an about 1.5 hour train ride to the city.

THE HIGH SCHOOL DOCTOR
The Underground Roadmap to 6, 7, and 8 Year
Accelerated/Combined Medical Programs (BA/MD) in the United States

Stevens Institute of Technology — UMDNJ - New Jersey Medical School (MD)
Office of Admissions
New Jersey Medical School
C-653 MSB
185 South Orange Avenue
Newark, NJ 07103-2714
(201)982-4631

Stevens Institute of Technology
Undergraduate Academic Rating: ***
Social Atmosphere Rating: **
Tuition of the Undergraduate Campus: $$$
Prestige of Associated Medical School: ***
Overall Rating of Combined Program: 78

PROGRAM TITLE:
BA/MD Program
7 year program

OPEN TO IN/OUT STATE STUDENTS:
Both in/out state students.

MINIMUM HIGH SCHOOL REQUIREMENTS:
GPA: Top 10% of Class
SAT: 1400
ACT: n/a

MINIMUM UNDERGRADUATE REQUIREMENTS:
GPA: 3.20
MCAT: National Mean

APPLICATION DEADLINE:
December 15

Stevens Institute of Technology is a private institution located in Hoboken, New Jersey. It is not only close to New York City, it is also home of Frank Sinatra. Last year, 56% of the approximately 2,1000 applicants gained admittance to the university. From the academic standpoint, Stevens Institute of Technology is mainly a school for those interested in technology and engineering. Like most private institution, the professors teach all of the classes at Stevens Institute of Technology. However, there is not a lot of flexibility in the choice of classes you can pick your first two years of college. This university enforces a mandatory course load for its first and second year students. The average class size of a regular course is between 20 and 25, while its faculty to student ratio is close to 10 to 1. Although it is a technology-orientated school, many students complain about the computer facilities and the lack of a good library on campus.

In terms of composition of the student body, there is ethnic diversity on campus; however, the majority of the students who attend this university are mostly male.

In terms of a social life on campus, thirty-five percent of the student body is a member of the Greek system. Along with the Greek system, there are 50 groups and organizations students can choose from ranging from jazz band to photography. However, most of the student body migrates to the gym, or they participate in the eighteen intramural sports the school has to offer.

With regards to living in Hoboken, many students enjoy the fact that they live so close to New York City. They also enjoy the bar scene and the food that Hoboken has to offer. However, the majority of the New Jersey students tend to go home on the weekend.

Tufts University – Tufts University School of Medicine
136 Harrison Avenue
Boston, Massachusetts 02111
(617) 636-6571
(Open only to Sophomores of Tufts University)

Tufts University
Undergraduate Academic Rating: ****
Social Atmosphere Rating: *****
Tuition of the Undergraduate Campus: $$$$
Prestige of Associated Medical School: ****
Overall Rating of Combined Program: 93

PROGRAM TITLE:
BA/MD Program
7 year program

OPEN TO IN/OUT STATE STUDENTS:
Both in/out state students.

MINIMUM HIGH SCHOOL REQUIREMENTS:
GPA: No Minimum
SAT: No Minimum
ACT: No Minimum

MINIMUM UNDERGRADUATE REQUIREMENTS:
GPA: 3.50
MCAT: Must Score National Mean

APPLICATION DEADLINE:
December 15

Tufts University is a private institution located in Medford, Massachusetts. Medford is about five miles northwest from the city of Boston. Although the academic reputation has only been known in the Northeast, the school is gaining popularity due to its growing reputation and its location. Last year, over 13,000 high school seniors applied to Tufts University with only 32% of them gaining admittance.

What struck us about Tufts University is the fact that 99% of the classes are taught by the professors. In fact, many Tufts University students rate their professor high in terms of accessibility and competence. Similar to most private universities, the average class size is small, and the student to faculty ratio is reasonably at 13 to 1. One of the negatives at Tufts University is the fact that the university places a lot of prerequisites that first year students have to take like World Civilization. Similar to Boston, the ethnic diversity at Tufts University is very pervasive.

With regards to on campus activities, Students describe on campus life as very active. Although Greek life is not that pervasive at Tufts where only 15% of the men and 3% of the women joining the Greek system, students also have the choice of over 150 activities. These activities range from working for the school newspaper to being a member of the debate team.

If and when a student gets tired of the college life in Medford, most of the students take the "T" Metro systems to Boston for more of a nightlife. Although there are on campus fraternity parties on campus, most of the action is in Boston where there is a bevy of bars and clubs one can choose from.

Union College — Albany Medical College
47 New Scotland Avenue
Albany, New York 12208
(518) 262-5521

Union College

Undergraduate Academic Rating: ****
Social Atmosphere Rating: ***
Tuition of the Undergraduate Campus: $$$$
Prestige of Associated Medical School: ***
Overall Rating of Combined Program: 84

PROGRAM TITLE:
BA/MD Program
8 year program

OPEN TO IN/OUT STATE STUDENTS:
Both in/out state students.

MINIMUM HIGH SCHOOL REQUIREMENTS:
GPA: No minimum
SAT: No minimum
ACT: No minimum

MINIMUM UNDERGRADUATE REQUIREMENTS:
GPA: 3.20
MCAT: Not needed

APPLICATION DEADLINE:
December 1

Union College is a private institution located in Schenectady, New York. Last year, around 4,000 applicants applied to Union College with around 47% of these applicants gaining admittance. At Union College, many of the students rate their professors as popular and available to the student body when needed. Unlike most schools, Union College goes by the Trimester system. Some students like it. Some don't. The students who like the Trimester system feel that they can concentrate and focus on three courses in one period of time instead of four or five.

The students who don't like it feel that the classes move at a pace quicker than they are used to. Plus, they complain about the fact that they have to study for final examinations three times per year. In terms of class size, the average is around 24, and the student to faculty ratio is 11 to 1. Although Union College is know as an engineering school, many students enjoy the fact that there is a variety of courses and classes they can choose from. As for as living in Schenectady, many students wished they lived somewhere else.

As for as life on campus, the Greek system is very prevalent in the social scene at Union College. About 30% of the student body belongs either to a fraternity or sorority. Although there is a strong Greek culture on campus, Union College does offer other campus events such as Parents weekend and Women's Week. Students are also interested in their intramural and intercollegiate sports. Similar to Rensselaer Polytechnic Institute, Union College enjoys its ice hockey as well.

University of Akron — **tern Ohio Universities College of Medicine**
4209 State Route 44
P.O. Box 95
Rootstown, Ohio 44272
(330)-325-2511

University of Akron
Undergraduate Academic Rating: ***
Social Atmosphere Rating: **
Tuition of the Undergraduate Campus: $
Prestige of Associated Medical School: ***
Overall Rating of Combined Program: 78

PROGRAM TITLE:
BA/MD Program
6 year program

OPEN TO IN/OUT STATE STUDENTS:
Both in/out state students.

MINIMUM HIGH SCHOOL REQUIREMENTS:
GPA: No Minimum
SAT: No Minimum
ACT: No Minimum

MINIMUM UNDERGRADUATE REQUIREMENTS:
GPA: 3.25
MCAT: Must Score an 8 on each section

APPLICATION DEADLINE:
December 15

The University of Akron is a public institution located in Akron, Ohio. Akron is 35 miles south of Cleveland. Last year, 44% of the approximately 6,900 high school seniors gained admittance to this university. Academically speaking, the University of Akron had seven undergraduate divisions that offer up to 154 undergraduate majors. The University of Akron also fields one of the largest computer centers in the state of Ohio. At this university, the student to faculty ratio is 16 to 1, while the average class size is 22. As for as ethnic diversity on campus is concerned, about 20% of the student body is a minority.

In terms of Greek life on campus, there are 17 fraternities and 5 sororities on campus. However, less than 5% of the student body is a member of the Greek system. But, the university does offer over 190 student groups or organizations to choose from ranging from the Society of Women Engineers to Society of Students in Construction. These student organizations along with the administration help field annual events such as International Fair and May Day. For other forms of entertainment, some students have gone to the Pro Football Hall of Fame in Canton, Ohio, the National Inventors Hall of Fame, and the Goodyear World of Rubbers.

University of Alabama –
University of Alabama School of Medicine
UAB Office of Enrollment Management
272 Hill University Center
Birmingham, AL 35294
(205) 934-8152

University of Alabama
Undergraduate Academic Rating: ***
Social Atmosphere Rating: **
Tuition of the Undergraduate Campus: $
Prestige of Medical School: **
Overall Score of Combined Program: 72

PROGRAM TITLE:
BA/MD Program
8 year program

OPEN TO IN/OUT STATE STUDENTS:
Both in/out state students.

MINIMUM HIGH SCHOOL REQUIREMENTS:
GPA: 3.5
SAT: 1250
ACT: 28

MINIMUM UNDERGRADUATE REQUIREMENTS:
GPA: 3.3 overall; 3.5 in all science classes
MCAT: Not needed

APPLICATION DEADLINE:
December 15

The University of Alabama is a public institution located in Tuscaloosa, Alabama. Last year, 80% of the 8,000 applicants gained admittance. Similar to most state schools, the campus is very large and TA's teach some of the introductory courses. Although the student to faculty ratio is around 25 to 1, many students have responded that their professors are very approachable and friendly.

The Greek life on campus dominates the social scene with 16% of the male undergraduates are in a fraternity and about 20% of the female undergraduates are in a sorority. If you were looking for a diverse student population, it would be difficult to fulfill that requirement here. About 85% of the undergraduate student body is Caucasion. Due to the lack of diversity, many students have felt uncomfortable with the college scene in Tuscaloosa.

As mentioned earlier, Greek life is a large component at the University of Alabama. It is also no secret that Alabama Football plays a prevalent part of most undergraduate lives as well. In fact, the Alabama-Auburn football game is still the most heated rivalry in all of college spots. The closet city near Tuscaloosa is Birmingham, which is about 1 ½ hour drive.

NAGENDRA SAI KONERU, M.D.
VINEET ARORA, M.D.
OMAR WANG, ATC

University of California at Riverside – University of California – Los Angeles School of Medicine
Biomedical Sciences Program
Los Angeles, California 90095
(310)-787-4333

University of California-Riverside
Undergraduate Academic Rating: ***
Social Atmosphere Rating: ***
Tuition of the Undergraduate Campus: $$ (out of state); $ (in state)
Prestige of Associated Medical School: ****
Overall Rating of Combined Program: 86

PROGRAM TITLE:
BA/MD Program
8 year program

OPEN TO IN/OUT STATE STUDENTS:
Both in/out state students.

MINIMUM HIGH SCHOOL REQUIREMENTS:
GPA: 3.50
SAT: 1050
ACT: n/a

MINIMUM UNDERGRADUATE REQUIREMENTS:
GPA: 3.50
MCAT: National Mean

APPLICATION DEADLINE:
December 15

The University of California-Riverside is a public institution located 60 miles east of Los Angeles. Of the total undergraduate enrollment, 99% of the student body is from California. It is no secret that UC-Riverside is not a powerhouse when it comes to academic strength compared to UC-Berkeley or UCLA. Therefore, gaining admittance to UC-Riverside is not as difficult as the other schools just mentioned. However, for you, the prospective medical student, the lure of UC-Riverside is the seven-year BS/MD program. UC-Riverside is also known for its research.

Thus, it is normal for some upper class students to participate in major innovative research projects. The average class size at UC-Riverside is 19. However, TA's was still teaching most of the upper-tier courses. Like the state of California, there is no question there is a lot of ethnic diversity on campus with Asian Americans representing 41% of the student population. However, most of the students feel that each of the ethnic groups on campus tend to stick together.

With regards to the social scene, the city of Riverside itself offers very little in terms of bar or club scene. Although there is a reasonably strong Greek life on campus, most of the students find Riverside quite boring. In terms of school spirit, many students feel that it is on life support or needs mouth-to-mouth resuscitation. Consequently, many students take road trips to Los Angeles or go to the beach to relieve some stress from school. If you like to ski, ski resorts like Big Bear are also within reasonable driving distance.

> University of Miami –
> University of Miami School of Medicine
> P.O. Box 248025
> Coral Gables, FL 33124
> (305)284-4323
> (state residents only)

University of Miami
Undergraduate Academic Rating: ****
Social Atmosphere Rating: *****
Tuition of the Undergraduate Campus: $$$
Prestige of Associated Medical School: ***
Overall Rating of Combined Program: 87

PROGRAM TITLE:
BA/MD Program
7 year program

OPEN TO IN/OUT STATE STUDENTS:
Both in/out state students.

MINIMUM HIGH SCHOOL REQUIREMENTS:
GPA: 3.5
SAT: 1360
ACT: 31

MINIMUM UNDERGRADUATE REQUIREMENTS:
GPA: 3.4
MCAT: National Mean

APPLICATION DEADLINE:
December 15

The University of Miami is a private institution located in Coral Cables, Florida. Coral Gables is about ten minutes without traffic from downtown Miami, and about ten to fifteen minutes from South Beach without traffic. There really isn't much to complain about in terms of the weather. Except for the hurricane season in September and October, the weather is sunny pretty much everyday there. Like the south Florida area, the campus is just beautiful. Although the University of Miami has been know as a jock school for its eight NCAA national championship between the football and baseball teams respectively since 1980, the school has a strong academic reputation as well.

Due to its location and reputation, over 12,000 applicants apply each year with about half of them gaining admittance. The average class size is about 14. The University of Miami also carries a good professor accessibility rating. In terms of student life, the campus is very diverse. Lots of students from the University of Miami are from different backgrounds. The athletic and educational facilities are also top-notch.

Similar to the campus, Miami is a diverse city with plenty of things to do. Out of all the cities in the United States, you will be hard pressed to find a better nightlife. From hotspots like South Beach and Coconut Grove to university sporting events on campus and professional sporting events off campus, one would have a tough time getting bored at U of M. In fact, if the scene in Miami gets to old, you can always travel to Key West, which is about 3 ½ hours away from campus. You might want to go on Halloween where the city has the biggest masquerade and costume party on Duval Street.

NAGENDRA SAI KONERU, M.D.
VINEET ARORA, M.D.
OMAR WANG, ATC

> **University of Michigan –
> University of Michigan School of Medicine**
> Interflex Program
> 5113 Medical Science I Building, Wing C
> Ann Arbor, MI 48109-0611
> (313)764-9534

University of Michigan
Undergraduate Academic Rating: ****
Social Atmosphere Rating: ****
Tuition of the Undergraduate Campus: $$$ (out of state); $ (in state)
Prestige of Associated Medical School: *****
Overall Rating of Combined Program: 92

PROGRAM TITLE:
Interflex Program
7 year program

OPEN TO IN/OUT STATE STUDENTS:
Both in/out state students.

MINIMUM HIGH SCHOOL REQUIREMENTS:
GPA: 3.5
SAT: 1350
ACT: 30

MINIMUM UNDERGRADUATE REQUIREMENTS:
GPA: 3.3
MCAT: National Mean

APPLICATION DEADLINE:
December 15

The University of Michigan is a public institution located in Ann Arbor, Michigan. Last year, over 21,000 applicants applied to U of M with only 64% of the applicants making the cut. Of the applicants who did gain admittance and accepted to go the University of Michigan, two-thirds of them were from Michigan. Thus, it is more difficult for out of state high school applicants to get in.

Like most state schools, the majority of the freshman/sophomore classes are extraordinary large and will be taught by TA's. However, as you get into your preferred major, the class size will a lot smaller and the availability and accessibility of your professor will be a lot higher. In fact, the average class size at U of M is around 28. In terms of on campus facilities, many of the students find it to be the biggest asset of the university.

At U of M, students are actively involved in all facets of life. About 20% of the undergraduate student body is a member of the Greek system. In fact, there are 37 national fraternities and 21 national sororities at U of M. Along with the Greek system, the university offers its athletically inclined students with a large array of intramural sports to participate in.

With regards to the social scene, Ann Arbor is the classic "college town". Although there is a fraternity party on campus each and every weekend, there are other alternatives a student can choose from. The bars on South University and Main Street are easily accessible either by care or within walking distance depending on where you live. (Author's Note: The hotspots we recommend are Touchdown's Bar and Grill, Rick's Café, Scorekeepers, Nectarine, Mitch's Place, and the Backroom.) If the bar scene doesn't suit your fancy, there is always concerts being played at Hill Auditorium.

University of Missouri-Columbia — University of Missouri-Columbia School of Medicine
Conley Scholars Program
One Hospital Drive, Columbia, Missouri 65212
University of Missouri-Columbia
(573) 882-2923
(Only for In State Students)

University of Missouri-Columbia
Undergraduate Academic Rating: ***
Social Atmosphere Rating: ***
Tuition of the Undergraduate Campus: $
Prestige of Associated Medical School: ****
Overall Rating of Combined Program: 85

PROGRAM TITLE:
Conley Scholars Program
8 year program

OPEN TO IN/OUT STATE STUDENTS:
Both in/out state students.

MINIMUM HIGH SCHOOL REQUIREMENTS:
GPA: 3.50
SAT: 1300
ACT: 30

MINIMUM UNDERGRADUATE REQUIREMENTS:
GPA: 3.30
MCAT: Not Needed

APPLICATION DEADLINE:
December 15

The University of Missouri-Columbia is a public institution located in Columbia, Missouri. It is about 2 hours away from both Kansas City and Saint Louis. Last year, of the over 9,000 high school seniors who applied to the university, about 90% of them gained full admittance. Similar to most large state universities, the university offers an extraordinary large amount of degree programs a freshman student can choose from. One of the strongest academic programs on campus is its Journalism/Communication program. Despite its large size, many students rate their professors high in accessibility and being knowledgeable about their subject material. At the university, the student to faculty ratio is only 10 to 1. The University of Missouri-Columbia is mainly composed of in state students (83 Percent).

However, many minority students note that they wished that the campus had more ethnic diversity. With regards to Greek life, about twenty-five percent of the student body is a member of the Greek system. In fact, the University of Missouri-Columbia has one of the largest Greek systems in the country. Although the Greek life is strong here, there are over 350 student groups on campus one can join. The university also has a strong intramural sports program to its "weekend warriors".

At Columbia, many students feel that there is a lot to do on campus. Along with the fraternity parties, some students choose to hike in areas just out of town or read a book in the many on campus parks that are readily available. If you are seeking a dance club like atmosphere, we recommend that you go to either Déjà vu or Tonic nightclub. Of course, if the club life doesn't fit the bill, there are a number of bars and pubs one can choose from.

University of Missouri Kansas City — University of Missouri Kansas City School of Medicine

School of Medicine
Council on Selection
2411 Holmes
Kansas City, MO 64108
(816)235-1870

University of Missouri-Kansas City

Undergraduate Academic Rating: **
Social Atmosphere Rating: ***
Tuition of the Undergraduate Campus: $$ (out of state); $ (in state)
Prestige of Associated Medical School: ***
Overall Rating of Combined Program: 78

PROGRAM TITLE:
BA/MD Program
6 year program

OPEN TO IN/OUT STATE STUDENTS:
Both in/out state students.

MINIMUM HIGH SCHOOL REQUIREMENTS:
GPA: 3.5
SAT: 1250
ACT: 29

MINIMUM UNDERGRADUATE REQUIREMENTS:
GPA: 3.3
MCAT: National Mean

APPLICATION DEADLINE:
December 15

The University of Missouri-Kansas City is a public institution located in Kansas City, Missouri. Last year, 68% of the approximately 2,600 applicants received admittance. From the academic side of the coin, the university offers over 80 undergraduate majors ranging from Accounting to Urban Affairs. The student to faculty ratio is 7 to 1.

On average, the class size is around 24. At UMKC, 80% of the student body is from Missouri. However, there are minority organizations on campus such as the Chinese Scholar and Student Association and the India Student Association. Seventy-four percent of the undergraduates are white. Many of the students hear note the excellent academic facilities and resources that are available to them.

As far as the Greek life on campus, there are four fraternities and three sororities on campus. About five percent of the student population belongs to the Greek system. Consequently, there is not much a Greek life here as it is in other major universities. There are over 100 student organizations to join on campus. Popular on campus events includes the Spring Fling and the International Food and Culture night. With regards to the nightlife, most students go to Westport, a large area of bars and clubs just on the outskirts of Kansas City. Many students also enjoy going to Kauffman Stadium to catch a Royals baseball game or to Arrowhead Stadium to try to catch a Chiefs football game. However, Chief tickets are tough to come by.

THE HIGH SCHOOL DOCTOR
The Underground Roadmap to 6, 7, and 8 Year
Accelerated/Combined Medical Programs (BA/MD) in the United States

> **University of Rochester –
> University of Rochester School of Medicine**
> Program Coordinator
> Rochester Early Medical Scholars
> Meliora Hall
> Rochester, NY 14627
> (716)275-3221

University of Rochester
Undergraduate Academic Rating: ***
Social Atmosphere Rating: *
Tuition of the Undergraduate Campus: $$$$
Prestige of Associated Medical School: *****
Overall Rating of Combined Program: 84

PROGRAM TITLE:
REMS Program
8 year program

OPEN TO IN/OUT STATE STUDENTS:
Both in/out state students.

MINIMUM HIGH SCHOOL REQUIREMENTS:
GPA: Top 3% of Class
SAT: 1400
ACT: 33
SAT II: 700

MINIMUM UNDERGRADUATE REQUIREMENTS:
GPA: 3.5
MCAT: Not needed

APPLICATION DEADLINE:
December 15

The University of Rochester is a private institution located in Rochester, New York. It is about 70 miles east of Niagara Falls and about 125 miles east of Toronto. Last year, just over 8,600 applicants applied to the University of Rochester with around two thirds of the applicant pool gaining admittance to the university.

At the University of Rochester, despite the cold weather, many students enjoy their academic experiences here. Although the course load and homework can be heavy, many students enjoy the 175 degree programs the school has to offer, and the fact that the university under certain circumstances will allow a student to take an additional year to take other classes for free. Yes, tuition is for free. On average, the class size is around 20, and the student to faculty ratio is around 11 to 1. Although many students feel that they have a wonderful library, they would like to see their athletic facilities upgraded.

As far as ethnic diversity on campus, many African Americans and Hispanics feel they are underrepresented. However, in general, many of the student body feels that everyone is very accepting of each other's racial differences. With regards to housing on campus, some students feel that they are quite comfortable and adequate. With regards to what to do on campus, there are over 150 groups or organizations to join ranging dance to art club. As far as having a Greek life, it is pretty dominate here at the University of Rochester. Twenty-five percent of the men belong to a fraternity where as 14% of the women belong to a sorority.

NAGENDRA SAI KONERU, M.D.
VINEET ARORA, M.D.
OMAR WANG, ATC

> **University of South Alabama –**
> **South Alabama School of Medicine**
> Office of Admissions
> Administrative Building, Room 182
> Mobile, AL 36688-0002
> (800)872-5247

University of South Alabama
Undergraduate Academic Rating: **
Social Atmosphere Rating: *
Tuition of the Undergraduate Campus: $
Prestige of Medical School: **
Overall score of combined program: 70

PROGRAM TITLE:
BA/MD Program
8 year program

OPEN TO IN/OUT STATE STUDENTS:
Both in/out state students.

MINIMUM HIGH SCHOOL REQUIREMENTS:
GPA: 3.5
SAT: 1250
ACT: 28

MINIMUM UNDERGRADUATE REQUIREMENTS:
GPA: 3.5
MCAT: Must score national mean

APPLICATION DEADLINE:
December 15

The University of South Alabama is located in Mobile, Alabama. It is a public institution with the majority of its students coming from Alabama. Last year, a whopping 93% of the school's applicants gained admittance to USA. AS you can see, the requirements of getting into this institution are not that taxing. Although USA is a public institution, the student to faculty ration is only 13 to 1. In terms of Greek life, around 10% of the student population belongs either in a fraternity or sorority.

The South Alabama commuter is not much of social scene.

"I wasn't happy with the fact that the campus was largely a commuter campus."
-Sara Summy, Sophomore

University of is more of a campus. So, there an on campus

Like the University of Alabama, there is not much diversity on campus where only 15% of the undergraduate student population is composed of Asian Americans, African-Americans, and Latinos. However the city of Mobile does offer a wonderful array of historical sites. Historical exhibits such as the U.S.S. Alabama Battleship Memorial Park and the Museum of Mobil are certainly must places to go sometime during your tenure at Mobile.

THE HIGH SCHOOL DOCTOR
The Underground Roadmap to 6, 7, and 8 Year
Accelerated/Combined Medical Programs (BA/MD) in the United States

University of Southern California – University of Southern California School of Medicine
College of Letters, Arts and Sciences
University of Southern California
CAS 100, University Park
Los Angeles, California 90089-0152
(213) 740-5930

University of Southern California
Undergraduate Academic Rating: ****
Social Atmosphere Rating: *****
Tuition of the Undergraduate Campus: $$$$
Prestige of Medical School: ***
Overall rating of combined program: 85

PROGRAM TITLE:
PIBBS
7 year program

OPEN TO IN/OUT STATE STUDENTS:
Both in/out state students.

MINIMUM HIGH SCHOOL REQUIREMENTS:
GPA: 3.75
SAT: 1300
ACT: n/a

MINIMUM UNDERGRADUATE REQUIREMENTS:
GPA: 3.5
MCAT: Must score national mean

APPLICATION DEADLINE:
January 15

USC is a private institution located in Los Angeles, California. USC is located deep in the heart of South Central. Despite the high crime rate in this area, many students find the campus security to be quite adequate. Because of the university is located in Los Angeles and its athletic reputation, USC has no trouble in receiving applications. Last year, over 26,000 applicants applied to USC with only 37% of them gaining admittance. At USC, you will also find a wide array of different ethnic backgrounds, however, many of the ethnic groups tend to keep to themselves. Although USC is a private institution, it pretty much acts and is run like a big state university. The school not only has wonderful athletic and computer facilities, USC offers a wide variety of majors for the prospective student.

In terms of social life, the on campus scene is dominated by the Greek system. In fact, many students feel it may be too big. With regards to living in Los Angeles, not many students have any complaints. The weather is beautiful and the bar and club scene speaks for itself. You can drive to Hollywood or go to the beach. Boredom is not option at USC. (Authors' Note: We recommend that you rent the movie *Swingers* to get a better feel for the nightlife in LA.)

Finally, USC has one of the strongest collegiate athletic programs in the country and the student support for its athletic program is tremendous. Although the USC Football teams in recent years have not been successful as it has been in the past, many students still get geared up for the USC-UCLA football rivalry each year.

University of Wisconsin at Madison – University of Wisconsin at Madison Medical School

Medical Scholars Program
1300 University Avenue, Room 1250
Madison, WI 53706
(608)263-7561
(state residents only)

University of Wisconsin-Madison

Undergraduate Academic Rating: ****
Social Atmosphere Rating: ****
Tuition of the Undergraduate Campus: $$
Prestige of Associated Medical School: ****
Overall Rating of Combined Program: 91

PROGRAM TITLE:
Medical Scholars Program
8 year program

OPEN TO IN/OUT STATE STUDENTS:
Both in/out state students.

MINIMUM HIGH SCHOOL REQUIREMENTS:
GPA: 3.80
SAT: 1300
ACT: 30

MINIMUM UNDERGRADUATE REQUIREMENTS:
GPA: 3.00
MCAT: Not needed

APPLICATION DEADLINE:
January 15

University of Wisconsin is a public institution located in Madison, Wisconsin. Last year, approximately 16,800 applications were received with 72% of the applicant pool gaining admittance. This university has eight undergraduate colleges and offers around 140 undergraduate majors. Many students who first dome to this university were mildly surprised with the quality of education they have received. On average, the class size is around 30, while the student to faculty ratio is 12 to 1. Like most large public institutions, there is a lot of bureaucratic "b.s." a student has to go through from registering for classes to looking for your professor on campus. The students on campus rated the athletic and academic facilities high by their standards. However, there is not much diversity on campus. Minorities only represent 10% of the student body.

As for as extracurricular activities on campus, there are over 700 campus organizations that a student can join. As far as a Greek life on campus, it is very active here, however, it is not a dominant part of the social life. Students enjoy participating in the over 25 intramural sports that the university has to offer. Most of the students would agree that sports are very important to the students and to the local residents of Madison. Along with the recent success of the football team, men's ice hockey, men's basketball, and the men's soccer team has also gained a lot of support from the student body.

Villanova University — MCP/Hahnemann School of Medicine

Office of Undergraduate Admissions
Villanova University
800 Lancaster Avenue
Villanova, PA 19085-1699
1-800-338-7927

Villanova University

Undergraduate Academic Rating: ****
Social Atmosphere Rating: ****
Tuition of the Undergraduate Campus: $$$
Prestige of the Associated Medical School: ****
Overall Rating of the Program: 86

PROGRAM TITLE:
BA/MD Program
6 year program

OPEN TO IN/OUT STATE STUDENTS:
Both in/out state students.

MINIMUM HIGH SCHOOL REQUIREMENTS:
GPA: 3.50
SAT: 1360
ACT: n/a

MINIMUM UNDERGRADUATE REQUIREMENTS:
GPA: 3.50
MCAT: National mean

APPLICATION DEADLINE:
December 15

Villanova University is a private Roman Catholic institution located in Villanova, Pennsylvania. It is about 12 miles west of downtown Philadelphia. Last year, just over 10,000 high school seniors applied to Villanova University with just over half of them gaining admittance. Many students ate Villanova state that they enjoy the fact that the most of their classes were taught by professors, instead of graduate students. In fact, the majority of the professors were graded high in terms of the quality on how they taught. At Villanova, the average class size is around 23, while the student to faculty ratio was 13 to 1. Villanova University also offers a wide assortment of courses with finance and accounting being the popular majors. Students on campus are mostly white and Catholic. About 10% of the student body is either African-American, Hispanic, or Asian American.

As far as extracurricular activities go, there are over 100 groups a student can choose from. Intramural sports are also popular among the students. Students also enjoy the Greek scene where 18% of the men and 34% of the women are members of either a fraternity or sorority respectively. However, you don't' have to be a member of the Greek system to party. Many students say they go to bars on Lancaster Avenue to hang out and socialize. Others may migrate at the Connelly Center. Considering that Philadelphia is close to Villanova, many students tend to go there for a better nightlife and to enjoy the cultural aspects of the city. The Jersey Shore and Atlantic City also await fro them, however, it is about a 2 hour drive from campus.

Virginia Commonwealth University – Virginia Commonwealth University School of Medicine
Guaranteed Admissions Programs
Honors Program
Anne L. Chandler, Ph.D.
920 W Franklin Street
PO Box 843010
Richmond, VA 23284-3010
(804) 828-1803

Virginia Commonwealth University
Undergraduate Academic Rating: ***
Social Atmosphere Rating: ***
Tuition of the Undergraduate Campus: $$
Prestige of Associated Medical School: ***
Overall Rating of Combined Program: 80

PROGRAM TITLE:
BA/MD Program
8 year program

OPEN TO IN/OUT STATE STUDENTS:
Both in/out state students.

MINIMUM HIGH SCHOOL REQUIREMENTS:
GPA: 3.00
SAT: 1270
ACT: 29

MINIMUM UNDERGRADUATE REQUIREMENTS:
GPA: 3.50
MCAT: Not needed

APPLICATION DEADLINE:
December 17

VCU is a public institution located in Richmond, Virginia. Last year, over 7,000 high students applied to VCU. About 75% of the applicants gained admittance to the university. Here at VCU, many students generally enjoy the looks and the resources on campus. However, starting in fall of 2001, all freshman students are "encouraged" a personal computer on campus even though the computer facilities are open 24 hours a day. Academically speaking, there are twelve undergraduate schools at VCU, where the student to faculty ratio is 18 to 1. The most popular majors on campus are psychology and biology. In terms of ethnic diversity, minorities represent about one-third of the undergraduate population at VCU.

In terms of Greek life on campus, less than 4% of the total undergraduate student body is a member of either a fraternity or sorority. However, there are over 170 groups and organizations you can join. Many students also participate in the ten intramural sports that VCU offers to both its male and female students.

As far as the nightlife goes in Richmond, there are fraternity parties on-campus, however, there is a decent club scene downtown. Places to go on our list are Club Fahrenheit, Catch 22, and Club Razzles. If the fraternity parties or the club life isn't pleasing, you can always go see the Richmond Riverfront or catch a Richmond Braves game, the AAA affiliate of the Atlanta Braves.

Youngstown University — Northeastern Ohio Universities College of Medicine

4209 State Route 44
P.O. Box 95
Rootstown, Ohio 44272
(330)-325-2511

Youngstown State University
Undergraduate Academic Rating: ***
Social Atmosphere Rating: ***
Tuition of the Undergraduate Campus: $$
Prestige of Associated Medical School: ***
Overall Rating of Combined Program: 80

PROGRAM TITLE:
BA/MD Program
6 year program

OPEN TO IN/OUT STATE STUDENTS:
Both in/out state students.

MINIMUM HIGH SCHOOL REQUIREMENTS:
GPA: None
SAT: None
ACT: None

MINIMUM UNDERGRADUATE REQUIREMENTS:
GPA: 3.25
MCAT: Must score at least 8 on each section

APPLICATION DEADLINE:
December 15

Youngstown State University is a public institution in Youngstown, Ohio. It is about hour away from both city of Cleveland and Pittsburgh. Last year, about 88% of the approximately 3,800 high school seniors who applied gained admittance. Ninety percent of the 12,500 students are from Ohio. Academically speaking, the average class size on campus is 22 while the student to faculty ratio is 20 to 1. The university has six undergraduate schools that offer up to 110 undergraduate majors to its students. Although YSU is a fairly large institution, TA's only teach a small percentage of the introductory courses. As far as diversity goes, from the Asian American perspective, they represent less than 1% of the undergraduate student population.

As far as Greek life on campus, there are seven fraternities and seven sororities to join. However, less than 5% of the total undergraduate student body is Greek. The school also up to 140 activities or organizations for YSU students to join. Although the school's athletic program is not as well known as the other top universities in the country, YSU has one of the strongest Division I-AA football teams in the country. In fact, in the last ten years, the football team has brought in four national championships. For those who are athletically challenged, YSU offers 29 intramural sports to both men and women.

As for as nightlife goes, we suggest you take road trips to either Cleveland or Pittsburgh. In Pittsburgh, there is a bunch of clubs and bars in an area called the Strip District. While you are in Pittsburgh, you may want to catch a Pirates baseball game at the new PNC Park or a Steelers football game at the new Heinz Field. In Cleveland, the Flats area is where you find the all of the bars and nightclubs. With regards to places to hang out in Youngstown, Mill Creek Park or the Butler Institute of American Art are the places we recommend.

ENDRA SAI KONERU, M.D.
NEET ARORA, M.D.
OMAR WANG, ATC

Chapter 16

The Best Accelerated Medical Programs

> *You do not merely want to be considered just the best of the best. You want to be considered the only one who does what you do.*
>
> *- Jerry Garcia*

The authors felt that it would not be accurate to make one rank list of the best accelerated medical programs for several reasons. The quality of the accelerated (BA/MD) program can be best measured by the quality of the medical school associated with the program. However, if you are stuck with a great medical school and a sub-par undergraduate university, the overall program may not be as valuable to you. There are so many variables that are important when looking at accelerated medical programs that when ranking them, one should rank them according to specific criteria. The following are rank lists according to criteria that many students we have talked to felt were important. The rank lists are not in order of importance and the schools listed are also not listed in order of importance.

The Top 5 Most Competitive Accelerated (BA/MD) Programs:
Northwestern University
Rice University
Brown University
Boston University
Case Western Reserve University
Special Mention:
Penn State University,
New York University,
and UCLA

THE HIGH SCHOOL DOCTOR
The Underground Roadmap to 6, 7, and 8 Year Accelerated/Combined Medical Programs (BA/MD) in the United States

The Top 5 Most Diverse Accelerated (BA/MD) Programs:
Rutgers University
UCLA
University of Missouri-Kansas City
University of Miami
Rice University

The Top 5 Accelerated (BA/MD) Programs with the Best Social Atmosphere:
Northwestern University
Boston University
University of Miami
UCLA
New York University
*Special Mention:
University of Michigan
University of Wisconsin
George Washington University

The Top 5 Accelerated (BA/MD) Programs with the Best Medical Schools as Counterpart
Rice University – Baylor Medical School
Northwestern University – Northwestern University School of Medicine
University of Rochester – University of Rochester School of Medicine
New York University – New York University School of Medicine
Case Western Reserve University – Case Western Reserve University School of Medicine

NAGENDRA SAI KONERU, M.D.
VINEET ARORA, M.D.
OMAR WANG, ATC

Chapter 17

The Future of Medicine

By Nagendra Sai Koneru, M.D.

The last years of Albert Einstein were spent with introspective analysis of the most profound questions. Einstein wanted to answer the most intriguing question of humankind. What was the equation for the existence of humankind? Through his genius in physics, Einstein went through endless equations in his dying days, hoping that he would ultimately find the unifying theory that tied all of existence together. Unfortunately, his efforts for this noble task ended unfulfilled.

The question is still being asked today. Why are we here? How are we here? As science progresses, new answers are uncovered, bringing us closer to that truth. The human genome project has given us the knowledge of every gene of a human's DNA. This knowledge can better help us understand the mechanisms of every disease known to mankind. Furthermore, perhaps the information from the human genome project will one day lead to the prevention of the myriad of diseases known to mankind.

For thousands, perhaps millions of years, religions have given us their own explanations on the meaning of life. Ancient sciences such as yoga and meditation have been used in the east as the gateway to heaven on earth. The east believes in the union between mind, body, and soul. According to the east, we are literally talking to our DNA everyday through the language of emotion and desire.

The west, on the other hand, has been devoted to the scientific method for the past century as the gold standard for finding the truth. Western medicine, in the allopathic sense, has been focused on treatment specific to the location of the disorder. A wholistic approach has just recently been gaining attention.

As science progresses one would probably conclude that the gap between the spirituality of the east and the scientific ideology of the west would only grow. However, quite the opposite has been playing out. As eastern ideas are being researched beyond the superficial rituality, deep hidden truths have been found. Yoga and meditation have been studied deeply using western methods. The results found have been fascinating. Perhaps there is a bridging between the gaps?

Deepak Chopra and Dharma Khalsa are examples of two physicians who believe in the bridging of the gaps. Dr. Dharma Khalsa is a board certified Anesthesiologist who decided to explore the ideas of the Sikh religion. His research led him to yoga and meditation. The experiences he had with yoga and meditation led him on a revolutionary path. He currently has his own clinic in Arizona where he has successfully documented the treatment of patients with AIDS, cancer, and Alzheimer's disease through the practice of yoga, meditation and self-empowering mantras.

Dr. Deepak Chopra, who you are probably already familiar with, has taken a similar route. He was an endocrinologist at Massachusetts General Hospital when he was attracted to the ideas of the east and Ayurvedic medicine. Dr. Chopra also has many documented examples of successful treatment with the use of eastern techniques.

What does the success of eastern medicine tell us? Perhaps, it tells us that disease is not external, but rather internal. Perhaps, disease is at the soul level or in western words, at the level of our genes. Perhaps techniques such as yoga and meditation and the chanting of certain of certain mantras help us get in touch with our own natural "vibrations" which is the language to communicate with own unique DNA.

What is the future of medicine? Change. I believe there will be a paradigm shift in the coming years. As medicine moves from the macro to the micro level, the words "genes" and "DNA" will become everyday language. However, this will only be the beginning. The study of the micro will propel us to dive into the submicro. We will again look at atoms, subatoms, quarks, and vibrations. We will once again be on the same page that Einstein was during his final days. This time we will look at the equations through the eyes of medicine. Perhaps our vision will be better able to see the answers.

NAGENDRA SAI KONERU, M.D.
VINEET ARORA, M.D.
OMAR WANG, ATC

APPENDIX A

State Government Contact Info Concerning Financial Aid

Alabama
> Alabama Commission on Higher Education
> P.O. Box 30200
> Montgomery, AL 36130
> Tel: 1-334-242-2274

Alaska
> Alaska Commission on Postsecondary Education
> 3030 Vintage Blvd
> Juneau, AK 99801
> Tel: 1-907-465-2962

Arizona
> Arizona Commission for Postsecondary Education
> 2020 N. Central, Suite 275
> Phoenix, AZ 85004
> Tel: 1-602-229-2590

Arkansas
> Arkansas Department of Higher Education
> 114 East Capitol
> Little Rock, AR 72201
> Tel: 1-501-371-2000

California
> California Student Aid Commission
> P.O. Box 510845
> Sacramento, CA 94245
> Tel: 1-916-445-0880

Colorado
> Colorado Commissions on Higher Education
> 1300 Broadway, 2nd Floor
> Denver, CO 80203
> Tel: 1-303-866-2723

NAGENDRA SAI KONERU, M.D.
VINEET ARORA, M.D.
OMAR WANG, ATC

Connecticut
    Department of Higher Education
    61 Woodland St.
    Hartford, CT 06105
    Tel: 1-860-566-8118

Delaware
    Commission of Higher Education
    Carvel State Office Bldg
    820 N. French St.
    Wilmington, DE 19801
    Tel: 1-302-577-3240

District of Columbia
    Office of Postsecondary Education
    2100 Martin Luther King Jr., Ave, SE
    Suite 401
    Washington D.C., 20020
    Tel: 1-202-727-3685

Florida
    Florida Office of Student Financial Assistance
    255 Collins
    Tallahassee, FL 32399
    Tel: 1-904-488-1034

Georgia
    Student Finance Commission
    2082 E. Exchange Place, Suite 200
    Atlanta, GA 30084
    Tel: 1-770-414-3006

Hawaii
    Systems Group
    641-18th Ave, V201
    Honolulu, HI 96816
    Tel: 1-808-733-9124

Idaho
    Office of the State Board of Education
    P.O. Box 83720
    Boise, ID 83720-0037
    Tel: 1-208-334-2270

Illinois
> Illinois Student Assistance Commission
> 1755 Lake Cook Dr.
> Deerfield, IL 60015
> Tel: 1-708-948-8550

Indiana
> State Student Assistance Commission of Indiana
> 150 W. Market St., Suite 500
> Indianapolis, IN 46204
> Tel: 1-317-232-2350

Iowa
> Iowa College of Student Aid Commission
> 200 Tenth, 4th Floor
> Des Moines, IA 50309-3609
> Tel: 1-515-281-3501

Kansas
> Kansas Board of Regents
> 700 SW Harrison, Suite 1410
> Topeka, KS 66603
> Tel: 1-913-296-3517

Kentucky
> Kentucky Higher Assistance Authority
> 1050 U.S. 127 South
> Frankfurt, KY 40601
> Tel: 1-502-564-7990

Louisiana
> Office of Student Financial Assistance
> P.O. Box 91202
> Baton Rouge, LA 70821
> Tel: 1-504-922-1011

Maine
> Financial Authority of Maine
> Maine Educational Assistance Division
> 119 State House Station
> One Weston Court
> Augusta, ME 04333
> Tel: 1-800-228-3734

NAGENDRA SAI KONERU, M.D.
VINEET ARORA, M.D.
OMAR WANG, ATC

Maryland
    Maryland Higher Education Committee
    State Scholarship Administration
    The Jeffrey Bldg
    16 Francis Street, Suite 209
    Annapolis, MD 21401
    Tel: 410-974-5370

Massachusetts
    Board of Regents of Higher Education
    Scholarship Office
    330 Stuart Street
    Boston, MA 02116
    Tel: 1-617-727-9420

Michigan
    Michigan Department of Education
    Student Financial Assistance Services
    Higher Education Authority
    P.O. Box 30462
    Lansing, MI 48909
    Tel: 1-517-373-3394

Minnesota
    Minnesota Higher Education Programs
    Capitol Square Bldg
    Suite 400
    550 Cedar Street
    St. Paul, MN 55101
    Tel: 1-612-296-3974

Mississippi
    Mississippi Institute of Higher Education
    3825 Ridgewood Rd.
    Jackson, MS 39211
    Tel: 601-982-6663

Missouri
    Missouri Board of Higher Education
    P.O. Box 1438
    3515 Amazonia Street
    Jefferson City, MO 65109
    Tel; 1-573-751-2361

Montana
> Office of the Commissions of Higher Education
> P.O. box 20301
> Helena, MT 59620
> Tel: 406-444-6594

Nebraska
> Nebraska Coordinating Commission For Post Secondary Education
> 140 N. Eighth Street
> Suite 300
> P.O. Box 95005
> Lincoln, NE 68508
> Tel: 1-402-471-2847

Nevada
> Nevada Department of Education
> Student Incentive Grant Program
> 700 E. 5th Street
> Carson City, NV 98701
> Tel: 1-702-687-9200

New Hampshire
> New Hampshire Postsecondary Education Commission
> 2 Industrial Park Drive
> Concord, NH 03301
> Tel: 1-603-271-2555

New Jersey
> New Jersey Department of Higher Education
> Office of Student Assistance
> 4 Quakerbridge Plaza, CN 540
> Trenton, NJ 08625
> Tel: 1-609-588-3288

New Mexico
> New Mexico Commission on Higher Education
> 1068 Cerillos Road
> Sante Fe, NM 87501
> Tel: 1-505-827-7383

North Carolina
> North Carolina State Educational Assistance Authority
> P.O. Box 2688
> Chapel Hill, NC 27515

NAGENDRA SAI KONERU, M.D.
VINEET ARORA, M.D.
OMAR WANG, ATC

    Tel: 1-919-549-8614

North Dakota
    University Systems
    600 E. Boulevard
    Bismark, ND 58505
    Tel: 1-701-328-2961

Ohio
    Ohio Board of Regents
    Ohio Student Aid Commissions
    State Grants and Scholarships Department
    309 S. 4th Street
    P.O. Box 182452
    Columbus, OH 43218
    Tel: 1-614-466-7420

Oklahoma
    Oklahoma State Regents for Higher Education
    500 Education Bldg
    State Capitol Complex
    Oklahoma City, OK 73105
    Tel: 1-405-524-9100

Oregon
    Oregon State Scholarship Commission
    1500 Valley River Dr., Suite 100
    Eugene, OR 97401
    Tel: 1-503-687-7400

Pennsylvania
    Pennsylvania Higher Education Assistance Agency
    1200 N. 7th Street
    Harrisburg, PA 17102
    Tel: 1-717-720-2850

Rhode Island
    Rhode Island Higher Education Assistance Authority
    560 Jefferson Blvd
    Warwick, RI 02886
    Tel: 1-401-736-1100

South Carolina
    South Carolina Commission on Higher Education

1333 Maine Street, Suite 200
Columbia, SC 29201
Tel: 1-803-737-2260

South Dakota

South Dakota Department of Educational and Cultural Affairs
Office of the Secretary
7000 Governors Drive
Pierre, SD 57051
1-605-773-3134

Tennessee

Tennessee Student Assistance Corporation
404 James Robertson Parkway
Suite 1950, Parkway Towers
Nashville, TN 37243
Tel: 1-615-741-1346

Texas

Texas Coordinating Board of Higher Education
Box 12788, Capitol Station
Austin, TX 78711
Tel: 1-512-483-6100

Utah

Utah Systems of Higher Education
355 West North Temple
3 Triad, Suite 550
Salt Lake City, UT 84180
Tel: 1-801-321-7100

Vermont

Vermont Student Assistance Corporation
P.O. Box 2000
Champlain Mill
Winooski, VT 05404
1-800-798-8722

Virginia

Virginia State Council of Higher Education
Office of Financial Aid
James Monroe Bldg
101 N. 14th Street, 10th Floor
Richmond, VA 23219

NAGENDRA SAI KONERU, M.D.
VINEET ARORA, M.D.
OMAR WANG, ATC

    Tel: 1-804-786-4690

Washington
    Higher Education Coordinating Board
    917 Lakeridge Way
    P.O. Box 43430
    Olympia, WA 98504
    Tel: 1-360-753-7800

West Virginia
    West Virginia Higher Education Program
    1018 Kanwaha Blvd. East
    Suite 700
    Charleston, WV 25301
    Tel: 1-304-558-4614

Wisconsin
    State of Wisconsin Higher Educational Aids Board
    P.O. Box 7885
    Madison, WI 53707
    Tel: 1-608-267-2206

Wyoming
    Wyoming Department of Higher Education
    Hathaway Bldg.
    Cheyenne, WY 82002
    Tel: 1-307-777-6213

APPENDIX B

Summer Programs for High School Students

1) Center for Mathematics, Science and Technology (CMST)
   Location: University of Maryland Eastern Shore, *Westminister, MD*

2) Center for Talented Youth (CTY)
   Location: Johns Hopkins University, *Baltimore, MD*
   Web site: http://www.jhu.edu/gifted/ctysummer/catalogs/os

3) COSMOS: California State Summer School for Mathematics and Science
   Location: University of California *3 campus locations - UC Davis, UC Irvine, UC Santa Cruz*
   Web site: http://www.ucop.edu/cosmos/

4) High School Honors Science/Mathematics Program
   Location: Michigan State University, *East Lansing, MI*
   Web site: http://www.dsme.msu.edu/outreach.html

5) Mathcamp
   Location: Mathematics Foundation of America, *Location varies*
   Web site: http://www.mathcamp.org/

6) Michigan Math and Science Scholars
   Location: University of Michigan, *Ann Arbor, MI*
   Web site: http://www.math.lsa.umich.edu/mmss

7) Program in Mathematics for Young Scientists (PROMYS)
   Location: Boston University, *Boston, MA*
   Web site: http://www.promys.org

8) Rutgers Young Scholars Program in Discrete Mathematics
   Location: Rutgers University-New Brunswick, *Piscataway, NJ*
   Web site: http://dimacs.rutgers.edu/ysp/

9) Stanford University Mathematics Camp (SUMaC)
   Location: Stanford University, *Stanford, CA*
   Web site: http://math.stanford.edu/sumac

10) Summer Program in Mathematics and Engineering for Gifted and High-Achieving Students
   Location: University of South Florida, *Tampa, FL*
   Web site: http://www.math.usf.edu

11) Summer Science Program in the Ojai Valley
   Location: Happy Valley School, *Ojai Valley, Southern California*
   Web site: http://www.summerscience.org/

12) UConn Mentor Connection
   Location: University of Connecticut, *Storrs, CT*
   Web site: http://www.gifted.uconn.edu/mentoruc.html

13) University of Chicago Young Scholars Program
   Location: University of Chicago, *Chicago, IL*
   Web site: http://www.uchicago.edu/docs/comm-outreach/programs/young-scholars.html

APPENDIX C

The *Underground* Vocabulary Builder

abase v. To lower in position, estimation, or the like; degrade.
abdicate v. To give up (royal power or the like).
abduction n. A carrying away of a person against his will, or illegally.
aberration n. Deviation from a right, customary, or prescribed course.
abet v. To aid, promote, or encourage the commission of (an offense).
abeyance n. A state of suspension or temporary inaction.
abhorrence n. The act of detesting extremely.
abhorrent adj. Very repugnant; hateful.
abject adj. Sunk to a low condition.
abjure v. To recant, renounce, repudiate under oath.
ablution n. A washing or cleansing, especially of the body.
abnegate v. To renounce (a right or privilege).
abominable adj. Very hateful.
abomination n. A very detestable act or practice.
aboriginal adj. Primitive; unsophisticated.
abrade v. To wear away the surface or some part of by friction.
abrasion n. That which is rubbed off.
abridge v. To make shorter in words, keeping the essential features, leaning out minor particles.
absolution n. Forgiveness, or passing over of offenses.
absolve v. To free from sin or its penalties.
abstain v. To keep oneself back (from doing or using something).
abstemious adj. Characterized by self denial or abstinence, as in the use of drink, food.
abstinence n. Self denial.
abstruse adj. Dealing with matters difficult to be understood.
abundant adj. Plentiful.
abusive adj. Employing harsh words or ill treatment.
abut v. To touch at the end or boundary line.
abyss n. Bottomless gulf.
accede v. To agree.
accession n. Induction or elevation, as to dignity, office, or government.
accost v. To speak to.
achromatic adj. Colorless, .
acme n. The highest point, or summit.
acoustic adj. Pertaining to the act or sense of hearing.
acquaint v. To make familiar or conversant.
acquiesce v. To comply; submit.

acquiescence n. Passive consent.
acquit v. To free or clear, as from accusation.
acquaintance n. Release or discharge from indebtedness, obligation, or responsibility.
acreage n. Quantity or extent of land, especially of cultivated land.
acrid adj. Harshly pungent or bitter.
acrimonious adj. Full of bitterness.
acrimony n. Sharpness or bitterness of speech or temper.
actuary n. An officer, as of an insurance company, who calculates and states the risks and premiums.
actuate v. To move or incite to action.
acumen n. Quickness of intellectual insight, or discernment; keenness of discrimination.
advent n. The coming or arrival, as of any important change, event, state, or personage.
advert v. To refer incidentally.
affable adj. Easy to approach.
affluence n. A profuse or abundant supply of riches.
affront n. An open insult or indignity.
agglomerate v. To pile or heap together.
aggrandize v. To cause to appear greatly.
aggregate n. The entire number, sum, mass, or quantity of something.
agrarian adj. Pertaining to land, especially agricultural land.
airy adj. Delicate, ethereal.
akin adj. Of similar nature or qualities.
alacrity n. Cheerful willingness.
albino n. A person with milky white skin and hair, and eyes with bright red pupil and usually pink iris.
alluvion n. Flood.
ally n. A person or thing connected with another, usually in some relation of helpfulness.
almanac n. A series of tables giving the days of the week together with certain astronomical information.
aloof adv. Not in sympathy with or desiring to associate with others.
alteration n. Change or modification.
altercate v. To contend angrily or zealously in words.
alternate n. One chosen to act in place of another, in case of the absence or incapacity of that other.
alternative n. Something that may or must exist, be taken or chosen, or done instead of something else.
altitude n. Vertical distance or elevation above any point or base-level, as the sea.
surprising or attacking the enemy.
ameliorate v. To relieve, as from pain or hardship
amenable adj. Willing and ready to submit.
anarchy n. Absence or utter disregard of government.
anathema n. Anything forbidden, as by social usage.
animosity n. Hatred.
annalist n. Historian.

annex v. To add or affix at the end.
annihilate v. To destroy absolutely.
annuity n. An annual allowance, payment, or income.
antenatal adj. Occurring or existing before birth.
anteroom n. A room situated before and opening into another, usually larger.
anthology n. A collection of extracts from the writings of various authors.
anticlimax n. A gradual or sudden decrease in the importance or impressiveness of what is said.
antiquate v. To make old or out of date.
antonym n. A word directly opposed to another in meaning.
anxious adj. Distressed in mind respecting some uncertain matter.
apathy n. Insensibility to emotion or passionate feeling.
aperture n. Hole.
apex n. The highest point, as of a mountain.
aphorism n. Proverb.
apiary n. A place where bees are kept.
apogee n. The climax.
apostasy n. A total departure from one's faith or religion.
apotheosis n. Deification.
arbitrary adj. Fixed or done capriciously.
arbitrate v. To act or give judgment as umpire.
arbor n. A tree.
archaic adj. Antiquated
archipelago n. Any large body of water studded with islands, or the islands collectively themselves.
asperity n. Harshness or roughness of temper.
aspirant n. One who seeks earnestly, as for advancement, honors, place.
astringent adj. Harsh in disposition or character.
astute adj. Keen in discernment.
atonement n. Amends, reparation, or expiation made from wrong or injury.
audacious adj. Fearless.
augment v. To make bigger...
auriferous adj. Containing gold.
aurora n. A luminous phenomenon in the upper regions of the atmosphere.
auspice n. favoring, protecting, or propitious influence or guidance.
austere adj. Severely simple; unadorned.
autonomous adj. Self-governing.
avarice n. Passion for getting and keeping riches.
azure n. The color of the sky.
baleful adj. Malignant.
bawl v. To proclaim by outcry.
belittle v. To disparage.
belle n. A woman who is a center of attraction because of her beauty, accomplishments, etc.

NAGENDRA SAI KONERU, M.D.
VINEET ARORA, M.D.
OMAR WANG, ATC

bellicose adj. Warlike.
belligerent adj. Manifesting a warlike spirit.
bemoan v. To lament
benediction n. a solemn invocation of the divine blessing.
benefactor n. A doer of kindly and charitable acts.
benevolent adj. Loving others and actively desirous of their well-being.
benign adj. Good and kind of heart.
blithe adj. Joyous.
boisterous adj. Unchecked merriment or animal spirits.
subjects.
boorish adj. Rude.
braggart n. A vain boaster.
brandish v. To wave, shake, or flourish triumphantly or defiantly, as a sword or spear.
brevity n. Shortness of duration.
brigand n. One who lives by robbery and plunder.
brusque adj. Somewhat rough or rude in manner or speech.
bumptious adj. Full of offensive and aggressive self-conceit.
bungle v. To execute clumsily.
buoyancy n. Power or tendency to float on or in a liquid or gas.
burnish v. To make brilliant or shining.
cacophony n. A disagreeable, harsh, or discordant sound or combination of sounds or tones.
caitiff adj. Cowardly.
cajole v. To impose on or dupe by flattering speech.
cajolery n. Delusive speech.
candid adj. Straightforward.
candor n. The quality of frankness or outspokenness.
capacious adj. Roomy.
capitulate v. To surrender or stipulate terms.
carnal adj. Sensual.
castigate v. To punish.
chagrin n. Keen vexation, annoyance, or mortification, as at one's failures or errors.
chameleon adj. Changeable in appearance.
charlatan n. A quack.
chateau n. A castle or manor-house.
chattel n. Any article of personal property.
check v. To hold back.
chiffon n. A very thin gauze used for trimmings, evening dress, etc.
chivalry n. The knightly system of feudal times with its code, usages and practices.
cholera n. An acute epidemic disease.
choleric adj. Easily provoked to anger.
choral adj. Pertaining to, intended for, or performed by a chorus or choir.
Christ n. A title of Jesus
christen v. To name in baptism.

Christendom n. That part of the world where Christianity is generally professed.
chromatic adj. Belonging, relating to, or abounding in color.
chronology n. The science that treats of computation of time or of investigation and arrangement of events.
chronometer n. A portable timekeeper of the highest attainable
claimant n. One who makes a claim or demand, as of right.
clairvoyance n. Intuitive sagacity or perception.
clamorous adj. Urgent in complaint or demand.
clan n. A tribe.
clandestine adj. Surreptitious.
clangor n. Clanking or a ringing, as of arms, chains, or bells; clamor.
clarify v. To render intelligible.
clarion n. A small shrill trumpet or bugle.
classify v. To arrange in a class or classes on the basis of observed resemblance's and differences.
clearance n. A certificate from the proper authorities that a vessel has complied with the law and may sail.
clemency n. Mercy.
clement adj. Compassionate.
close-hauled adj. Having the sails set for sailing as close to the wind as possible.
coercive adj. Serving or tending to force.
cogent adj. Appealing strongly to the reason or conscience.
cognate adj. Akin.
cognizant adj. Taking notice.
literary or scientific pursuits.
collapse v. To cause to shrink, fall in, or fail.
collapsible adj. That may or can collapse.
colleague n. An associate in professional employment.
collective adj. Consisting of a number of persons or objects considered as gathered into a mass, or sum.
collector n. One who makes a collection, as of objects of art, books, or the like.
collegian n. A college student.
collide v. To meet and strike violently.
collier n. One who works in a coal-mine.
collision n. Violent contact.
colloquial adj. Pertaining or peculiar to common speech as distinguished from literary.
colloquialism n. Form of speech used only or chiefly in conversation.
colloquy n. Conversation.
collusion n. A secret agreement for a wrongful purpose.
colossus n. Any strikingly great person or object.
comely adj. Handsome.
comestible adj. Fit to be eaten.
keeping.
competent adj. Qualified.

compunction n. Remorseful feeling.
concur v. To agree.
congenial adj. Having kindred character or tastes.
connoisseur n. A critical judge of art, especially one with thorough knowledge and sound judgment of art.
connubial adj. Pertaining to marriage or matrimony.
consanguineous adj. Descended from the same parent or ancestor.
conspicuous adj. Clearly visible.
contagious adj. Transmitting disease.
contaminate v. To pollute.
contemplate v. To consider thoughtfully.
contiguous adj. Touching or joining at the edge or boundary.
contingency n. Possibility of happening.
contingent adj. Not predictable.
said.
contraposition n. A placing opposite.
credence n. Belief.
credible adj. Believable.
credulous adj. Easily deceived.
curtail v. To cut off or cut short.
dearth n. Scarcity, as of something customary, essential ,or desirable.
affirmation.
decrepit adj. Enfeebled, as by old age or some chronic infirmity.
defalcate v. To cut off or take away, as a part of something.
degenerate v. To become worse or inferior.
deleterious adj. Hurtful, morally or physically.
delirious adj. Raving.
cleared up.
deprecate v. To express disapproval or regret for, with hope for the opposite.
despond v. To lose spirit, courage, or hope.
despondent adj. Disheartened.
diatribe n. A bitter or malicious criticism.
dictum n. A positive utterance.
didactic adj. Pertaining to teaching.
discord n. Absence of harmoniousness.
discountenance v. To look upon with disfavor.
disengage v. To become detached.
disfavor n. Disregard.
disfigure v. To impair or injure the beauty, symmetry, or appearance of.
dishabille n. Undress or negligent attire.
dishonest adj. Untrustworthy.
disillusion v. To disenchant.
durance n. Confinement.
duration n. The period of time during which anything lasts.

duteous adj. Showing submission to natural superiors.
dutiable adj. Subject to a duty, especially a customs duty.
dutiful adj. Obedient.
dwindle v. To diminish or become less.
dyne n. The force which, applied to a mass of one gram for 1 second, would give it a velocity of 1 cm/s.
earnest adj. Ardent in spirit and speech.
earthenware n. Anything made of clay and baked in a kiln or dried in the sun.
eatable adj. Edible.
ebullient adj. Showing enthusiasm or exhilaration of feeling.
eccentric adj. Peculiar.
eccentricity n. Idiosyncrasy.
eclipse n. The obstruction of a heavenly body by its entering into the shadow of another body.
economize v. To spend sparingly.
ecstasy n. Rapturous excitement or exaltation.
ecstatic adj. Enraptured.
edible adj. Suitable to be eaten.
edict n. That which is uttered or proclaimed by authority as a rule of action.
edify v. To build up, or strengthen, especially in morals or religion.
editorial n. An article in a periodical written by the editor and published as an official argument.
educe v. To draw out.
efface v. To obliterate.
effect n. A consequence.
effective adj. Fit for a destined purpose.
effectual adj. Efficient.
effeminacy n. Womanishness.
effeminate adj. Having womanish traits or qualities.
effervesce v. To bubble up.
effervescent adj. Giving off bubbles of gas.
effulgence n. Splendor.
electrolysis n. The process of decomposing a chemical compound by the passage of an electric current.
electrotype n. A metallic copy of any surface, as a coin.
elegy n. A lyric poem lamenting the dead.
emancipate v. To release from bondage.
embargo n. Authoritative stoppage of foreign commerce or of any special trade.
embark v. To make a beginning in some occupation or scheme.
embarrass v. To render flustered or agitated.
embellish v. To make beautiful or elegant by adding attractive or ornamental features.
embezzle v. To misappropriate secretly.
emblazon v. To set forth publicly or in glowing terms.
emblem n. A symbol.

expectorate v. To cough up and spit forth.
expediency n. Fitness to meet the requirements of a particular case.
expedient adj. Contributing to personal advantage.
expedite v. To hasten the movement or progress of.
expeditious adj. Speedy.
expend v. To spend.
expense n. The laying out or expending or money or other resources, as time or strength.
expiate v. To make satisfaction or amends for.
explicate v. To clear from involvement.
explicit adj. Definite.
explode v. To cause to burst in pieces by force from within.
explosion n. A sudden and violent outbreak.
explosive adj. Pertaining to a sudden and violent outbreak.
exposition n. Formal presentation.
expository adj. Pertaining to a formal presentation.
expostulate v. To discuss.
exposure n. An open situation or position in relation to the sun, elements, or points of the compass.
expressive adj. Full of meaning.
expulsion n. Forcible ejection.
extradition n. The surrender by a government of a person accused of crime to the justice of another government.
extrajudicial adj. Happening out of court.
extraneous adj. Having no essential relation to a subject.
extraordinary adj. Unusual.
extravagance n. Undue expenditure of money.
extravagant adj. Needlessly free or lavish in expenditure.
extremist n. One who supports extreme measures or holds extreme views.
extremity n. The utmost point, side, or border, or that farthest removed from a mean position.
extricate v. Disentangle.
extrude v. To drive out or away.
exuberance n. Rich supply.
exuberant adj. Marked by great plentifulness.
fabricate v. To invent fancifully or falsely.
fabulous adj. Incredible.
facet n. One of the small triangular plane surfaces of a diamond or other gem.
facetious adj. Amusing.
facial adj. Pertaining to the face.
facile adj. Not difficult to do.
facilitate v. To make more easy.
facility n. Ease.
facsimile n. An exact copy or reproduction.

faction n. A number of persons combined for a common purpose.
factious adj. Turbulent.
fallacious adj. Illogical.
fealty n. Loyalty.
feasible adj. That may be done, performed, or effected; practicable.
federate v. To league together.
feint n. Any sham, pretense, or deceptive movement.
felicitate v. To wish joy or happiness to, especially in view of a coming event.
felicity n. A state of well-founded happiness.
felon n. A criminal or depraved person.
felonious adj. Showing criminal or evil purpose.
felony n. One of the highest class of offenses, and punishable with death or imprisonment.
feminine adj. Characteristic of woman or womankind.
fernery n. A place in which ferns are grown.
ferocious adj. Of a wild, fierce, and savage nature.
flagrant adj. Openly scandalous.
flamboyant adj. Characterized by extravagance and in general by want of good taste.
fluctuation n. Frequent irregular change back and forth from one state or degree to another.
flue n. A smoke-duct in a chimney.
fluent adj. Having a ready or easy flow of words or ideas.
fluential adj. Pertaining to streams.
foppish adj. Characteristic of one who is unduly devoted to dress and the niceties of manners.
forbearance n. Patient endurance or toleration of offenses.
forby adv. Besides.
forcible adj. Violent.
forebode v. To be an omen or warning sign of, especially of evil.
forecast v. To predict.
forecastle n. That part of the upper deck of a ship forward of the after fore-shrouds.
foreclose v. To bar by judicial proceedings the equitable right of a mortgagor to redeem property.
forgery n. Counterfeiting.
fraternal adj. Brotherly.
frigidarium n. A room kept at a low temperature for preserving fruits, meat, etc.
frivolity n. A trifling act, thought, saying, or practice.
fugacious adj. Fleeting.
fulcrum n. The support on or against which a lever rests, or the point about which it turns.
fulminate v. To cause to explode.
fulsome adj. Offensive from excess of praise or commendation.
fumigate v. To subject to the action of smoke or fumes, especially for disinfection.
functionary n. An official.

NAGENDRA SAI KONERU, M.D.
VINEET ARORA, M.D.
OMAR WANG, ATC

fundamental adj. Basal.
fungible adj. That may be measured, counted, or weighed.
gauge n. An instrument for measuring.
gaiety n. Festivity.
gaily adv. Merrily.
gait n. Carriage of the body in going.
gallant adj. Possessing a brave or chivalrous spirit.
galvanism n. Current electricity, especially that arising from chemical action.
galvanize v. To imbue with life or animation.
gastronomy n. The art of preparing and serving appetizing food.
gendarme n. In continental Europe, particularly in France, a uniformed and armed police officer.
genealogy n. A list, in the order of succession, of ancestors and their descendants.
genealogist n. A tracer of pedigrees.
generality n. The principal portion.
generalize v. To draw general inferences.
generally adv. Ordinarily.
gesture n. A movement or action of the hands or face, expressive of some idea or emotion.
gratuitous adj. Voluntarily.
gratuity n. That which is given without demand or claim. Tip.
gravity n. Seriousness.
gregarious adj. Not habitually solitary or living alone.
guile n. Duplicity.
guileless adj. Frank.
gyroscope n. An instrument for illustrating the laws of rotation.
habitable adj. Fit to be dwelt in.
habitant n. Dweller.
habitual adj. According to usual practice.
habitude n. Customary relation or association.
hackney v. To make stale or trite by repetition.
haggard adj. Worn and gaunt in appearance.
halcyon adj. Calm.
hale adj. Of sound and vigorous health.
handwriting n. Penmanship.
hanger-on n. A parasite.
happy-go-lucky adj. Improvident.
harangue n. A tirade.
harass v. To trouble with importunities, cares, or annoyances.
harbinger n. One who or that which foreruns and announces the coming of any person or thing.
hard-hearted adj. Lacking pity or sympathy.
hardihood n. Foolish daring.
harmonious adj. Concordant in sound.

havoc n. Devastation.
hawthorn n. A thorny shrub much used in England for hedges.
hilarious adj. Boisterously merry.
hillock n. A small hill or mound.
hinder v. To obstruct.
hindmost adj. Farthest from the front.
hindrance n. An obstacle.
hirsute adj. Having a hairy covering.
hoard v. To gather and store away for the sake of accumulation.
hoarse adj. Having the voice harsh or rough, as from a cold or fatigue.
homage n. Reverential regard or worship.
homogeneity n. Congruity of the members or elements or parts.
homogeneous adj. Made up of similar parts or elements.
homologous adj. Identical in nature, make-up, or relation.
homonym n. A word agreeing in sound with but different in meaning from another.
homophone n. A word agreeing in sound with but different in meaning from another.
honorarium n. A token fee or payment to a professional man for services.
hoodwink v. To deceive.
horde n. A gathered multitude of human beings.
hosiery n. A stocking.
hospitable adj. Disposed to treat strangers or guests with generous kindness.
hospitality n. The practice of receiving and entertaining strangers and guests with kindness.
hostility n. Enmity.
huckster n. One who retails small wares.
humane adj. Compassionate.
humanitarian n. A philanthropist.
humanize v. To make gentle or refined.
humbug n. Anything intended or calculated to deceive or mislead.
humiliate v. To put to shame.
hydrodynamics n. The branch of mechanics that treats of the dynamics of fluids.
hydroelectric adj. Pertaining to electricity developed water or steam.
hydromechanics n. The mechanics of fluids.
hydrometer n. An instrument for determining the density of solids and
hypnosis n. An artificial trance-sleep.
hypnotic adj. Tending to produce sleep.
hypnotism n. An artificially induced somnambulistic state in which the mind readily acts on suggestion.
hypnotize v. To produce a somnambulistic state in which the mind readily acts on suggestions.
hypocrisy n. Extreme insincerity.
hypocrite n. One who makes false professions of his views or beliefs.
hypodermic adj. Pertaining to the area under the skin.
hypotenuse n. The side of a right-angled triangle opposite the right angle.

hypothesis n. A proposition taken for granted as a premise from which to reach a conclusion.
hysteria n. A nervous affection occurring typically in paroxysms of laughing and crying.
ichthyic adj. Fish-like.
ichthyology n. The branch of zoology that treats of fishes.
ichthyosaurs n. A fossil reptile.
icily adv. Frigidly.
iciness n. The state of being icy.
icon n. An image or likeness.
iconoclast n. An image-breaker.
idealize v. To make to conform to some mental or imaginary standard.
idiom n. A use of words peculiar to a particular language.
idiosyncrasy n. A mental quality or habit peculiar to an individual.
idolize v. To regard with inordinate love or admiration.
ignoble adj. Low in character or purpose.
ignominious adj. Shameful.
Iliad n. A Greek epic poem describing scenes from the siege of Troy.
illuminant n. That which may be used to produce light.
illuminate v. To supply with light.
illumine v. To make bright or clear.
illusion n. An unreal image presented to the senses.
illusive adj. Deceptive.
illusory adj. Deceiving or tending to deceive, as by false appearance.
imaginable adj. That can be imagined or conceived in the mind.
imaginary adj. Fancied.
imbibe v. To drink or take in.
imbroglio n. A misunderstanding attended by ill feeling, perplexity, or strife.
imbrue v. To wet or moisten.
imitation n. That which is made as a likeness or copy.
imitator n. One who makes in imitation.
immaculate adj. Without spot or blemish.
immaterial adj. Of no essential consequence.
immature adj. Not full-grown.
immeasurable adj. Indefinitely extensive.
immense adj. Very great in degree, extent, size, or quantity.
immerse v. To plunge or dip entirely under water or other fluid.
immersion n. The act of plunging or dipping entirely under water or another fluid.
immigrant n. A foreigner who enters a country to settle there.
immigrate v. To come into a country or region from a former habitat.
imminence n. Impending evil or danger.
imminent adj. Dangerous and close at hand.
immiscible adj. Separating, as oil and water.
immoral adj. Habitually engaged in licentious or lewd practices.
impecunious adj. Having no money.

impede v. To be an obstacle or to place obstacles in the way of.
impel v. To drive or urge forward.
impend v. To be imminent.
imperative adj. Obligatory.
imperceptible adj. Indiscernible.
imperfectible adj. That can not be perfected.
imperil v. To endanger.
imperious adj. Insisting on obedience.
impermissible adj. Not permissible.
impersonal adj. Not relating to a particular person or thing.
impersonate v. To appear or act in the character of.
impersuadable adj. Unyielding.
impertinence n. Rudeness.
inadmissible adj. Not to be approved, considered, or allowed, as testimony.
inadvertent adj. Accidental.
inadvisable adj. Unadvisable.
inane adj. Silly.
incandescence n. The state of being white or glowing with heat.
incandescent adj. White or glowing with heat.
incapacitate v. To deprive of power, capacity, competency, or qualification.
incapacity n. Want of power to apprehend, understand, and manage.
incarcerate v. To imprison.
incendiary n. Chemical or person who starts a fire-literally or figuratively.
incentive n. That which moves the mind or inflames the passions.
inception n. The beginning.
intrigue n. A plot or scheme, usually complicated and intended to accomplish something by secret ways.
intrinsic adj. Inherent.
introductory adj. Preliminary.
introgression n. Entrance.
introvert v. To turn within.
intrude v. To come in without leave or license.
last first.
irreparable adj. That can not be rectified or made amends for.
irrepressible adj. That can not be restrained or kept down.
irresistible adj. That can not be successfully withstood or opposed.
irresponsible adj. Careless of or unable to meet responsibilities.
irreverence n. The quality showing or expressing a deficiency of veneration, especially for sacred things.
irreverent adj. Showing or expressing a deficiency of veneration, especially for sacred things.
irreverential adj. Showing or expressing a deficiency of veneration, especially for sacred things.
irreversible adj. Irrevocable.

NAGENDRA SAI KONERU, M.D.
VINEET ARORA, M.D.
OMAR WANG, ATC

irrigant adj. Serving to water lands by artificial means.
irrigate v. To water, as land, by ditches or other artificial means.
irritable adj. Showing impatience or ill temper on little provocation.
irritancy n. The quality of producing vexation.
irritant n. A mechanical, chemical, or pathological agent of inflammation, pain, or tension.
irritate v. To excite ill temper or impatience in.
irruption n. Sudden invasion.
isle n. An island.
islet n. A little island.
isobar n. A line joining points at which the barometric pressure is the same at a specified moment.
isochronous adj. Relating to or denoting equal intervals of time.
laureate adj. Crowned with laurel, as a mark of distinction.
lave v. To wash or bathe.
lawgiver n. A legislator.
lawmaker n. A legislator.
lax adj. Not stringent or energetic.
laxative adj. Having power to open or loosen the bowels.
lea n. A field.
leaflet n. A little leaf or a booklet.
leaven v. To make light by fermentation, as dough.
leeward n. That side or direction toward which the wind blows.
left-handed adj. Using the left hand or arm more dexterously than the right.
legacy n. A bequest.
legalize v. To give the authority of law to.
legging n. A covering for the leg.
legible adj. That may be read with ease.
liturgy n. A ritual.
livelihood n. Means of subsistence.
livid adj. Black-and-blue, as contused flesh.
loam n. A non-coherent mixture of sand and clay.
loath adj. Averse.
loathe v. To abominate.
locative adj. Indicating place, or the place where or wherein an action occurs.
lucrative adj. Highly profitable.
ludicrous adj. Laughable.
luminary n. One of the heavenly bodies as a source of light.
luminescent adj. Showing increase of light.
luminescence n. Showing increase.
mandate n. A command.
mandatory adj. Expressive of positive command, as distinguished from merely directory.
mane n. The long hair growing upon and about the neck of certain animals, as the horse and the lion.

maneuver v. To make adroit or artful moves: manage affairs by strategy.
mania n. Insanity.
maniac n. a person raving with madness.
manifesto n. A public declaration, making announcement, explanation or defense of intentions, or motives.
manor n. The landed estate of a lord or nobleman.
mantel n. The facing, sometimes richly ornamented, about a fireplace, including the usual shelf above it.
mantle n. A cloak.
manumission n. Emancipation.
manumit v. To set free from bondage.
marine adj. Of or pertaining to the sea or matters connected with the sea.
maritime adj. Situated on or near the sea.
maroon v. To put ashore and abandon (a person) on a desolate coast or island.
martial adj. Pertaining to war or military operations.
Martian adj. Pertaining to Mars, either the Roman god of war or the planet.
martyrdom n. Submission to death or persecution for the sake of faith or principle.
masonry n. The art or work of constructing, as buildings, walls, etc., with regularly arranged stones.
masquerade n. A social party composed of persons masked and costumed so as to be disguised.
mediate v. To effect by negotiating as an agent between parties.
medicine n. A substance possessing or reputed to possess curative or remedial properties.
medieval adj. Belonging or relating to or descriptive of the middle ages.
mercenary adj. Greedy
merciful adj. Disposed to pity and forgive.
merciless adj. Cruel.
meretricious adj. Alluring by false or gaudy show.
mesmerize v. To hypnotize.
messieurs n. pl. Gentlemen.
metallurgy n. The art or science of extracting a metal from ores, as by smelting.
metamorphosis n. A passing from one form or shape into another.
metaphor n. A figure of speech in which one object is likened to another, by speaking as if the other.
metaphysical adj. Philosophical.
metropolitan adj. Pertaining to a chief city.
mettle n. Courage.
mettlesome adj. Having courage or spirit.
microcosm n. The world or universe on a small scale.
micrometer n. An instrument for measuring very small angles or dimensions.
microphone n. An apparatus for magnifying faint sounds.
microscope n. An instrument for assisting the eye in the vision of minute objects or features of objects.

microscopic adj. Adapted to or characterized by minute observation.
microscopy n. The art of examing objects with the microscope.
midsummer n. The middle of the summer.
midwife n. A woman who makes a business of assisting at childbirth.
mien n. The external appearance or manner of a person.
migrant adj. Wandering.
migrate v. To remove or pass from one country, region, or habitat to another.
mischievous adj. Fond of tricks.
miscount v. To make a mistake in counting.
miscreant n. A villain.
misdeed n. A wrong or improper act.
misdemeanor n. Evil conduct, small crime.
miser n. A person given to saving and hoarding unduly.
mishap n. Misfortune.
misinterpret v. To misunderstand.
mislay v. To misplace.
extraordinary liberality.
munificent adj. Extraordinarily generous.
muster n. An assemblage or review of troops for parade or inspection, or for numbering off.
narrate v. To tell a story.
navel n. The depression on the abdomen where the umbilical cord of the fetus was attached.
navigable adj. Capable of commercial navigation.
navigate v. To traverse by ship.
nectarine n. A variety of the peach.
needlework n. Embroidery.
needy adj. Being in need, want, or poverty.
nefarious adj. Wicked in the extreme.
negate v. To deny.
negation n. The act of denying or of asserting the falsity of a proposition.
neglectful adj. Exhibiting or indicating omission.
negligee n. A loose gown worn by women.
negligence n. Omission of that which ought to be done.
negligent adj. Apt to omit what ought to be done.
negligible adj. Transferable by assignment, endorsement, or delivery.
negotiable v. To bargain with others for an agreement, as for a treaty or transfer of property.
Nemesis n. A goddess; divinity of chastisement and vengeance.
neocracy n. Government administered by new or untried persons.
neo-Darwinsim n. Darwinism as modified and extended by more recent students.
neo-Latin n. Modernized Latin.
neopaganism n. A new or revived paganism.
Neolithic adj. Pertaining to the later stone age.

neology n. The coining or using of new words or new meanings of words.
neophyte adj. Having the character of a beginner.
nestle v. To adjust cozily in snug quarters.
nestling adj. Recently hatched.
nettle v. To excite sensations of uneasiness or displeasure in.
network n. Anything that presents a system of cross- lines.
neural adj. Pertaining to the nerves or nervous system.
neurology n. The science of the nervous system.
neuter adj. Neither masculine nor feminine.
Newtonian adj. Of or pertaining to Sir Isaac Newton, the English philosopher.
niggardly adj. Stingy. (no longer acceptable to use)
nihilist n. An advocate of the doctrine that nothing either exists or can be known.
nil n. Nothing
nimble adj. Light and quick in motion or action.
nit n. The egg of a louse or some other insect.
nocturnal adj. Of or pertaining to the night.
noiseless adj. Silent.
noisome adj. Very offensive, particularly to the sense of smell.
noisy adj. Clamorous.
nomad adj. Having no fixed abode.
nomic adj. Usual or customary.
nominal adj. Trivial.
nonpareil n. One who or that which is of unequaled excellence.
normalcy n. The state of being normal.
Norman adj. Of or peculiar to Normandy, in northern France.
nostrum n. Any scheme or recipe of a charlatan character.
noticeable adj. Perceptible.
notorious adj. Unfavorably known to the general public.
novellette n. A short novel.
novice n. A beginner in any business or occupation.
nowadays adv. In the present time or age.
nowhere adv. In no place or state.
noxious adj. Hurtful.
nuance n. A slight degree of difference in anything perceptible to the
obsequies n. Funeral rites.
obsequious adj. Showing a servile readiness to fall in with the wishes or will of another.
observance n. A traditional form or customary act.
observant adj. Quick to notice.
observatory n. A building designed for systematic astronomical observations.
obsolescence n. The condition or process of gradually falling into disuse.
obsolescent adj. Passing out of use, as a word.
obsolete adj. No longer practiced or accepted.
obstetrician n. A practitioner of midwifery.

obstetrics n. The branch of medical science concerned with the treatment and care of women during pregnancy.
obstinacy n. Stubborn adherence to opinion, arising from conceit or the desire to have one's own way.
obstreperous adj. Boisterous.
obstruct v. To fill with impediments so as to prevent passage, either wholly or in part.
obstruction n. Hindrance.
obtrude v. To be pushed or to push oneself into undue prominence.
obtrusive adj. Tending to be pushed or to push oneself into undue prominence.
obvert v. To turn the front or principal side of (a thing) toward any person or object.
obviate v. To clear away or provide for, as an objection or difficulty.
occasion n. An important event or celebration.
Occident n. The countries lying west of Asia and the Turkish dominions.
occlude v. To absorb, as a gas by a metal.
occult adj. Existing but not immediately perceptible.
occupant n. A tenant in possession of property, as distinguished from the actual owner.
occurrence n. A happening.
octagon n. A figure with eight sides and eight angles.
octave n. A note at this interval above or below any other, considered in relation to that other.
octavo n. A book, or collection of paper in which the sheets are so folded as to make eight leaves.
octogenarian adj. A person of between eighty and ninety years.
ocular adj. Of or pertaining to the eye.
oculist n. One versed or skilled in treating diseases of the eye.
oddity n. An eccentricity.
ode n. The form of lyric poetry anciently intended to be sung.
odious adj. Hateful.
odium n. A feeling of extreme repugnance, or of dislike and disgust.
odoriferous adj. Having or diffusing an odor or scent, especially an agreeable one.
odorous adj. Having an odor, especially a fragrant one.
off adj. Farther or more distant.
offhand adv. Without preparation.
officiate v. To act as an officer or leader.
officious adj. Intermeddling with what is not one's concern.
offshoot n. Something that branches off from the parent stock.
ogre n. A demon or monster that was supposed to devour human beings.
opalescence n. The property of combined refraction and reflection of light, resulting in smoky tints.
opaque adj. Impervious to light.
ostracism n. Exclusion from intercourse or favor, as in society or politics.
ostracize v. To exclude from public or private favor.
ought v. To be under moral obligation to be or do.

paramount adj. Supreme in authority.
paroxysm n. A sudden outburst of any kind of activity.
parricide n. The murder of a parent.
parse v. To describe, as a sentence, by separating it into its elements and describing each word.
parsimonious adj. Unduly sparing in the use or expenditure of money.
partible adj. Separable.
pentagon n. A figure, especially, with five angles and five sides.
pentahedron n. A solid bounded by five plane faces.
pentameter n. In prosody, a line of verse containing five units or feet.
pentathlon n. The contest of five associated exercises in the great games and the same contestants.
penultimate adj. A syllable or member of a series that is last but one.
penurious adj. Excessively sparing in the use of money.
periodicity n. The habit or characteristic of recurrence at regular intervals.
peripatetic adj. Walking about.
perjure v. To swear falsely to.
perjury n. A solemn assertion of a falsity.
permanence n. A continuance in the same state, or without any change that destroys the essential form or nature.
permanent adj. Durable.
perseverance n. A persistence in purpose and effort.
persevere v. To continue striving in spite of discouragements.
persiflage n. Banter.
persist v. To continue steadfast against opposition.
persistence n. A fixed adherence to a resolve, course of conduct, or the like.
personage n. A man or woman as an individual, especially one of rank or high station.
personal adj. Not general or public.
personality n. The attributes, taken collectively, that make up the character and nature of an individual.
personnel n. The force of persons collectively employed in some service.
practicable adj. Feasible.
prate v. To talk about vainly or foolishly.
prattle v. To utter in simple or childish talk.
preamble n. A statement introductory to and explanatory of what follows.
precarious adj. Perilous.
precise adj. Exact.
precision n. Accuracy of limitation, definition, or adjustment.
preclude v. To prevent.
precocious adj. Having the mental faculties prematurely developed.
profiteer n. One who profits.
profligacy n. Shameless viciousness.
profligate adj. Abandoned to vice.
profuse adj. Produced or displayed in overabundance.

progeny n. Offspring.
progression n. A moving forward or proceeding in course.
prohibition n. A decree or an order forbidding something.
prosaic adj. Unimaginative.
proscenium n. That part of the stage between the curtain and the orchestra.
proscribe v. To reject, as a teaching or a practice, with condemnation or denunciation.
proscription n. Any act of condemnation and rejection from favor and privilege.
proselyte n. One who has been won over from one religious belief to another.
prosody n. The science of poetical forms.
prospector n. One who makes exploration, search, or examination, especially for minerals.
prospectus n. A paper or pamphlet containing information of a proposed undertaking.
prostrate adj. Lying prone, or with the head to the ground.
protagonist n. A leader in any enterprise or contest.
proxy n. A person who is empowered by another to represent him or her in a given matter.
prudence n. Caution.
prudential adj. Proceeding or marked by caution.
pugnacious adj. Quarrelsome.
pupilage n. The state or period of being a student.
purgatory n. An intermediate state where souls are made fit for paradise or heaven by expiatory suffering.
qualification n. A requisite for an employment, position, right, or privilege.
qualify v. To endow or furnish with requisite ability, character, knowledge, skill, or possessions.
qualm n. A fit of nausea.
quandary n. A puzzling predicament.
quantity n. Magnitude.
quarantine n. The enforced isolation of any person or place infected with contagious disease.
quarrelsome adj. Irascible.
quarter n. One of four equal parts into which anything is or may be divided.
quarterly adj. Occurring or made at intervals of three months.
quartet n. A composition for four voices or four instruments.
Quixotic adj. Chivalrous or romantic to a ridiculous or extravagant degree.
rapine n. The act of seizing and carrying off property by superior force, as in war.
rapt adj. Enraptured.
raptorial adj. Seizing and devouring living prey.
ration v. To provide with a fixed allowance or portion, especially of food.
rationalism n. The formation of opinions by relying upon reason alone, independently of authority.
raucous adj. Harsh.
ravage v. To lay waste by pillage, rapine, devouring, or other destructive methods.
ravenous adj. Furiously voracious or hungry.

recant v. To withdraw formally one's belief (in something previously believed or maintained).
recapitulate v. To repeat again the principal points of.
recapture v. To capture again.
recede v. To move back or away.
recline v. To cause to assume a leaning or recumbent attitude or position.
recluse n. One who lives in retirement or seclusion.
reclusory n. A hermitage.
recognizance n. An acknowledgment entered into before a court with condition to do some particular act.
recognize v. To recall the identity of (a person or thing).
recoil v. To start back as in dismay, loathing, or dread.
recollect v. To recall the knowledge of.
reconcilable adj. Capable of being adjusted or harmonized.
reconnoiter v. To make a preliminary examination of for military, surveying, or geological purposes.
rectitude n. The quality of being upright in principles and conduct.
recuperate v. To recover.
recur v. To happen again or repeatedly, especially at regular intervals.
recure v. To cure again.
recurrent adj. Returning from time to time, especially at regular or stated intervals.
redemption n. The recovery of what is mortgaged or pledged, by paying the debt.
redolent adj. Smelling sweet and agreeable.
redolence n. Smelling sweet and agreeable.
redoubtable adj. Formidable.
redound n. Rebound.
redress v. To set right, as a wrong by compensation or the punishment of the wrong-doer.
rehabilitate v. To restore to a former status, capacity, right rank, or privilege.
reign v. To hold and exercise sovereign power.
reimburse v. To pay back as an equivalent of what has been expended.
rein n. A step attached to the bit for controlling a horse or other draft-animal.
reinstate v. To restore to a former state, station, or authority.
reiterate v. To say or do again and again.
rejoin v. To reunite after separation.
rejuvenate v. To restore to youth.
rejuvenescence n. A renewal of youth.
relapse v. To suffer a return of a disease after partial recovery.
relegate v. To send off or consign, as to an obscure position or remote destination.
relent v. To yield.
relevant adj. Bearing upon the matter in hand.
reliance n. Dependence.
reliant adj. Having confidence.
remission n. Temporary diminution of a disease.

remodel v. Reconstruct.
remonstrance n. Reproof.
repartee n. A ready, witty, or apt reply.
repeal v. To render of no further effect.
repel v. To force or keep back in a manner, physically or mentally.
repellent adj. Having power to force back in a manner, physically or mentally.
reproduction n. The process by which an animal or plant gives rise to another of its kind.
reproof n. An expression of disapproval or blame personally addressed to one censured.
repudiate v. To refuse to have anything to do with.
repugnance n. Thorough dislike.
repugnant adj. Offensive to taste and feeling.
resistless adj. Powerless.
resonance n. The quality of being able to reinforce sound by sympathetic vibrations.
resonance adj. Able to reinforce sound by sympathetic vibrations.
resonate v. To have or produce resonance.
resource n. That which is restored to, relied upon, or made available for aid or support.
respite n. Interval of rest.
resplendent adj. Very bright.
respondent adj. Answering.
restitution n. Restoration of anything to the one to whom it properly belongs.
resumption n. The act of taking back, or taking again.
resurgent adj. Surging back or again.
resurrection n. A return from death to life
resuscitate v. To restore from apparent death.
retaliate v. To repay evil with a similar evil.
retch v. To make an effort to vomit.
retention n. The keeping of a thing within one's power or possession.
reticence n. The quality of habitually keeping silent or being reserved in utterance.
reticent adj. Habitually keeping silent or being reserved in utterance.
retinue n. The body of persons who attend a person of importance in travel or public appearance.
retort n. A retaliatory speech.
retouch v. To modify the details of.
rotate v. To cause to turn on or as on its axis, as a wheel.
rote n. Repetition of words or sounds as a means of learning them, with slight attention.
rotund adj. Round from fullness or plumpness.
rudimentary adj. Being in an initial, early, or incomplete stage of development.
rue v. To regret extremely.
ruffian adj. A lawless or recklessly brutal fellow.
salutatory n. The opening oration at the commencement in American colleges.
salvage n. Any act of saving property.
salvo n. A salute given by firing all the guns, as at the funeral of an officer.

sanctimonious adj. Making an ostentatious display or hypocritical pretense of holiness or piety.
sanction v. To approve authoritatively.
sanctity n. Holiness.
sanguinary adj. Bloody.
sanguine adj. Having the color of blood.
sanguineous adj. Consisting of blood.
sapid adj. Affecting the sense of taste.
sapience n. Deep wisdom or knowledge.
sapient adj. Possessing wisdom.
sapiential adj. Possessing wisdom.
saponaceous adj. Having the nature or quality of soap.
sarcasm n. Cutting and reproachful language.
sarcophagus n. A stone coffin or a chest-like tomb.
sardonic adj. Scornfully or bitterly sarcastic.
satiate v. To satisfy fully the appetite or desire of.
satire n. The employment of sarcasm, irony, or keenness of wit in ridiculing vices.
satiric adj. Resembling poetry, in which vice, incapacity ,or corruption is held up to ridicule.
satirize v. To treat with sarcasm or derisive wit.
secant adj. Cutting, especially into two parts.
second-rate adj. Second in quality, size, rank, importance, etc.
secrecy n. Concealment.
secretary n. One who attends to correspondence, keeps records. or does other writing for others.
secretive adj. Having a tendency to conceal.
sedate adj. Even-tempered.
sedentary adj. Involving or requiring much sitting.
sediment n. Matter that settles to the bottom of a liquid.
sedition n. Conduct directed against public order and the tranquillity of the state.
seditious adj. Promotive of conduct directed against public order and the tranquillity of the state.
seduce v. To entice to surrender chastity.
sedulous adj. Persevering in effort or endeavor.
seer n. A prophet.
seethe v. To be violently excited or agitated.
sensorium n. The sensory apparatus.
sensual adj. Pertaining to the body or the physical senses.
sensuous adj. Having a warm appreciation of the beautiful or of the refinements of luxury.
sentence n. A related group of words containing a subject and a predicate and expressing a complete thought.
sentience n. Capacity for sensation or sense-perception.
sentient adj. Possessing the power of sense or sense-perception.

sentinel n. Any guard or watch stationed for protection.
significance n. Importance.
significant adj. Important, especially as pointing something out.
signification n. The meaning conveyed by language, actions, or signs.
similar adj. Bearing resemblance to one another or to something else.
simile n. A comparison which directs the mind to the representative object itself.
skeptic n. One who doubts any statements.
skepticism n. The entertainment of doubt concerning something.
skiff n. Usually, a small light boat propelled by oars.
skirmish n. Desultory fighting between advanced detachments of two armies.
sleight n. A trick or feat so deftly done that the manner of performance escapes observation.
slight adj. Of a small importance or significance.
slothful adj. Lazy.
sluggard n. A person habitually lazy or idle.
sociable adj. Inclined to seek company.
socialism n. A theory of civil polity that aims to secure the reconstruction of society.
socialist adj. One who advocates reconstruction of society by collective ownership of land and capital.
sociology n. The philosophical study of society.
Sol n. The sun.
somber adj. Gloomy.
somniferous adj. Tending to produce sleep.
somnolence n. Oppressive drowsiness.
somnolent adj. Sleepy.
sonata n. An instrumental composition.
sonnet n. A poem of fourteen decasyllabic or octosyllabiclines expressing two successive phrases.
sonorous adj. Resonant.
soothsayer n. One who claims to have supernatural insight or foresight.
spinster n. A woman who has never been married.
stanza n. A group of rimed lines, usually forming one of a series of similar divisions in a poem.
statecraft n. The art of conducting state affairs.
static adj. Pertaining to or designating bodies at rest or forces in equilibrium.
statics n. The branch of mechanics that treats of the relations that subsist among forces in order.
stationary adj. Not moving.
statistician n. One who is skilled in collecting and tabulating numerical facts.
statuesque adj. Having the grace, pose, or quietude of a statue.
statuette n. A figurine.
stature n. The natural height of an animal body.
statute n. Any authoritatively declared rule, ordinance, decree, or law.
stealth n. A concealed manner of acting.

stellar adj. Pertaining to the stars.
steppe n. One of the extensive plains in Russia and Siberia.
sterling adj. Genuine.
stifle v. To smother.
stigma n. A mark of infamy or token of disgrace attaching to a person as the result of evil-doing.
stiletto n. A small dagger.
stimulant n. Anything that rouses to activity or to quickened action.
stimulate v. To rouse to activity or to quickened action.
stimulus n. Incentive.
stingy adj. Cheap, unwilling to spend money.
stipend n. A definite amount paid at stated periods in compensation for services or as an allowance.
Stoicism n. The principles or the practice of the Stoics-being very even tempered in success and failure.
subconscious adj. Being or occurring in the mind, but without attendant consciousness or conscious perception.
subjacent adj. Situated directly underneath.
subjection n. The act of bringing into a state of submission.
subjugate v. To conquer.
subliminal adj. Being beneath the threshold of consciousness.
sublingual adj. Situated beneath the tongue.
submarine adj. Existing, done, or operating beneath the surface of the sea.
submerge v. To place or plunge under water.
submergence n. The act of submerging.
submersible adj. Capable of being put underwater.
submersion n. The act of submerging.
submission n. A yielding to the power or authority of another.
submittal n. The act of submitting.
subordinate adj. Belonging to an inferior order in a classification.
subsequent adj. Following in time.
subservience n. The quality, character, or condition of being servilely following another's behests.
subservient adj. Servilely following another's behests.
subside v. To relapse into a state of repose and tranquillity.
subsist v. To be maintained or sustained.
subsistence n. Sustenance.
substantive adj. Solid.
subtend v. To extend opposite to.
subterfuge n. Evasion.
subterranean adj. Situated or occurring below the surface of the earth.
miraculously or by the immediate exercise of divine power.
supernumerary adj. Superfluous.
supersede v. To displace.

supine adj. Lying on the back.
supplant v. To take the place of.
supple adj. Easily bent.
supplementary adj. Being an addition to.
supplicant n. One who asks humbly and earnestly.
surmount v. To overcome by force of will.
surreptitious adj. Clandestine.
surrogate n. One who or that which is substituted for or appointed to act in place of another.
surround v. To encircle.
surveyor n. A land-measurer.
susceptibility n. A specific capability of feeling or emotion.
susceptible adj. Easily under a specified power or influence.
suspense n. Uncertainty.
tacit adj. Understood.
taciturn adj. Disinclined to conversation.
tack n. A small sharp-pointed nail.
tact n. Fine or ready mental discernment shown in saying or doing the proper thing.
tactician n. One who directs affairs with skill and shrewdness.
tactics n. Any maneuvering or adroit management for effecting an object.
tangency n. The state of touching.
tangent adj. Touching.
tangible adj. Perceptible by touch.
tannery n. A place where leather is tanned.
tantalize v. To tease.
tantamount adj. Having equal or equivalent value, effect, or import.
tapestry n. A fabric to which a pattern is applied with a needle, designed for ornamental hangings.
tarnish v. To lessen or destroy the luster of in any way.
taut adj. Stretched tight.
taxation n. A levy, by government, of a fixed contribution.
temporary adj. Lasting for a short time only.
temporize v. To pursue a policy of delay.
terrify v. To fill with extreme fear.
territorial adj. Pertaining to the domain over which a sovereign state
theorist n. One given to speculating.
theorize v. To speculate.
transcribe v. To write over again (something already written)
transgress v. To break a law.
transience n. Something that is of short duration.
transparent adj. Easy to see through or understand.
transpire v. To come to pass.
transplant v. To remove and plant in another place.
transposition n. The act of reversing the order or changing the place of.

treble adj. Multiplied by three.
tripod n. A three-legged stand, usually hinged near the top, for supporting some instrument.
turgid adj. Swollen.
turpitude n. Depravity.
tutelage n. The act of training or the state of being under instruction.
tutelar adj. Protective.
tutorship n. The office of a guardian.
twinge n. A darting momentary local pain.
typical adj. Characteristic.
typify v. To serve as a characteristic example of.
typographical adj. Pertaining to typography or printing.
typography n. The arrangement of composed type, or the appearance of printed matter.
tyrannical adj. Despotic.
tyranny n. Absolute power arbitrarily or unjustly administrated.
tyro n. One slightly skilled in or acquainted with any trade or profession.
ubiquitous adj. Being present everywhere.
ulterior adj. Not so pertinent as something else to the matter spoken of.
ultimate adj. Beyond which there is nothing else.
ultimatum n. A final statement or proposal, as concerning terms or conditions.
umbrage n. A sense of injury.
unaccountable adj. Inexplicable.
unaffected adj. Sincere.
unanimous adj. Sharing the same views or sentiments.
unanimity n. The state or quality of being of one mind.
affairs.
undercharge v. To make an inadequate charge for.
underexposed adj. Insufficiently exposed for proper or full development, as negatives in photography.
undergarment n. A garment to be worn under the ordinary outer garments.
underman v. To equip with less than the full complement of men.
undersell v. To sell at a lower price than.
undersized adj. Of less than the customary size.
underhanded adj. Clandestinely carried on.
ungainly adj. Clumsy.
unguent n. Any ointment or lubricant for local application.
unicellular adj. Consisting of a single cell.
univalence n. Monovalency.
unify v. To cause to be one.
unique adj. Being the only one of its kind.
unison n. A condition of perfect agreement and accord.
unisonant adj. Being in a condition of perfect agreement and accord.
Unitarian adj. Pertaining to a religious body that rejects the doctrine of the Trinity.
unlawful adj. Illegal.

unlimited adj. Unconstrained.
unnatural adj. Artificial.
upbraid v. To reproach as deserving blame.
upcast n. A throwing upward.
upheaval n. Overthrow or violent disturbance of established order or condition.
upheave v. To raise or lift with effort.
uppermost adj. First in order of precedence.
uproarious adj. Noisy.
uproot v. To eradicate.
upturn v. To throw into confusion.
urban adj. Of, or pertaining to, or like a city.
urbanity n. Refined or elegant courtesy.
urchin n. A roguish, mischievous boy.
urgency n. The pressure of necessity.
usage n. Treatment.
usurious adj. Taking unlawful or exorbitant interest on money loaned.
usurp v. To take possession of by force.
vainglory n. Excessive, pretentious, and demonstrative vanity.
vale n. Level or low land between hills.
valediction n. A bidding farewell.
valedictorian n. Student who delivers an address at graduating exercises of an educational institution.
valedictory n. A parting address.
valid adj. Founded on truth.
valorous adj. Courageous.
vapid adj. Having lost sparkling quality and flavor.
vaporizer n. An atomizer.
variable adj. Having a tendency to change.
variance n. Change.
variant n. A thing that differs from another in form only, being the same in essence or substance.
variation n. Modification.
variegate v. To mark with different shades or colors.
vassal n. A slave or bondman.
vaudeville n. A variety show.
vegetal adj. Of or pertaining to plants.
vegetarian n. One who believes in the theory that man's food should be exclusively vegetable.
vegetate v. To live in a monotonous, passive way without exercise of the mental faculties.
vegetation n. Plant-life in the aggregate.
vegetative adj. Pertaining to the process of plant-life.
vehement adj. Very eager or urgent.
velocity n. Rapid motion.

velvety adj. Marked by lightness and softness.
venal adj. Mercenary, corrupt.
vendible adj. Marketable.
vendition n. The act of selling.
vendor n. A seller.
veneer n. Outside show or elegance.
venerable adj. Meriting or commanding high esteem.
venerate v. To cherish reverentially.
venereal adj. Pertaining to or proceeding from sexual intercourse.
venial adj. That may be pardoned or forgiven, a forgivable sin.
venison n. The flesh of deer.
venom n. The poisonous fluid that certain animals secrete.
venous adj. Of, pertaining to, or contained or carried in a vein or veins.
veracious adj. Habitually disposed to speak the truth.
veracity n. Truthfulness.
verbatim adv. Word for word.
verbiage n. Use of many words without necessity.
verbose adj. Wordy.
verdant adj. Green with vegetation.
verification n. The act of proving to be true, exact, or accurate.
verify v. To prove to be true, exact, or accurate.
verily adv. In truth.
verity n. Truth.
vermin n. A noxious or troublesome animal.
vernacular n. The language of one's country.
vernal adj. Belonging to or suggestive of the spring.
versatile adj. Having an aptitude for applying oneself to new and varied tasks or to various subjects.
version n. A description or report of something as modified by one's character or opinion.
vertex n. Apex.
vertical adj. Lying or directed perpendicularly to the horizon.
vertigo n. Dizziness.
vestige n. A visible trace, mark, or impression, of something absent, lost, or gone.
vestment n. Clothing or covering.
veto n. The constitutional right in a chief executive of refusing to approve an enactment.
vicarious adj. Suffered or done in place of or for the sake of another.
viceroy n. A ruler acting with royal authority in place of the sovereign in a colony or province.
vicissitude n. A change, especially a complete change, of condition or circumstances, as of fortune.
vie v. To contend.
vigilance n. Alert and intent mental watchfulness in guarding against danger.
vigilant adj. Being on the alert to discover and ward off danger or insure safety.

NAGENDRA SAI KONERU, M.D.
VINEET ARORA, M.D.
OMAR WANG, ATC

vignette n. A picture having a background or that is shaded off gradually.
vincible adj. Conquerable.
vindicate v. To prove true, right, or real.
vindicatory adj. Punitive.
vindicative adj. Revengeful.
vinery n. A greenhouse for grapes.
virulent adj. Exceedingly noxious or deleterious.
visage n. The face, countenence, or look of a person.
viscount n. In England, a title of nobility, ranking fourth in the order of British peerage.
vista n. A view or prospect.
visual adj. Perceptible by sight.
visualize v. To give pictorial vividness to a mental representation.
vitality n. The state or quality of being necessary to existence or continuance.
vitalize v. To endow with life or energy.
vitiate v. To contaminate.
vituperable adj. Deserving of censure.
vivacity n. Liveliness.
vivify v. To endue with life.
vivisection n. The dissection of a living animal.
vocable n. a word, especially one regarded in relation merely to its qualities of sound.
vocative adj. Of or pertaining to the act of calling.
vociferance n. The quality of making a clamor.
vociferate v. To utter with a loud and vehement voice.
vociferous adj. Making a loud outcry.
vogue n. The prevalent way or fashion.
volant adj. Flying or able to fly.
volatile adj. Changeable.
volition n. An act or exercise of will.
volitive adj. Exercising the will.
voluble adj. Having great fluency in speaking.
voluptuous adj. having fullness of beautiful form, as a woman, with or without sensuous or sensual quality.
voracious adj. Eating with greediness or in very large quantities.
wantonness n. Recklessness.
whet v. To make more keen or eager.
whimsical adj. Capricious.
whine v. To utter with complaining tone.
wholly adv. Completely.
wield v. To use, control, or manage, as a weapon, or instrument, especially with full command.
wile n. An act or a means of cunning deception.
winsome adj. Attractive.
wintry adj. Lacking warmth of manner.
wiry adj. Thin, but tough and sinewy.

witchcraft n. Sorcery.
witless adj. Foolish, indiscreet, or silly.
witling n. A person who has little understanding.
witticism n. A witty, brilliant, or original saying or sentiment.
wittingly adv. With knowledge and by design.
wizen v. To become or cause to become withered or dry.
wizen-faced adj. Having a shriveled face.
working-man n. One who earns his bread by manual labor.
workmanlike adj. Like or befitting a skilled workman.
workmanship n. The art or skill of a workman.
wrangle v. To maintain by noisy argument or dispute.
wreak v. To inflict, as a revenge or punishment.
wrest v. To pull or force away by or as by violent twisting or wringing.
wretchedness n. Extreme misery or unhappiness.
writhe v. To twist the body, face, or limbs or as in pain or distress.
writing n. The act or art of tracing or inscribing on a surface letters or ideographs.
wry adj. Deviating from that which is proper or right.
yearling n. A young animal past its first year and not yet two years old.
zealot n. One who espouses a cause or pursues an object in an immoderately partisan manner.
zeitgeist n. The intellectual and moral tendencies that characterize any age or epoch.
zenith n. The culminating-point of prosperity, influence, or greatness.
zephyr n. Any soft, gentle wind.
zodiac n. An imaginary belt encircling the heavens within which are the larger planets.

NAGENDRA SAI KONERU, M.D.
VINEET ARORA, M.D.
OMAR WANG, ATC

APPENDIX D

Postcards

The following pages will provide you with postcards that you can mail to the BA/MD programs. The postcards will save you countless hours of phonecalls and time. Make sure that you include your address on the top left corner of the postcard and the stamp amount necessary on the top right hand corner.

THE HIGH SCHOOL DOCTOR
The Underground Roadmap to 6, 7, and 8 Year
Accelerated/Combined Medical Programs (BA/MD) in the United States

**Binghamton University –
SUNY Health Sciences Center at Syracuse
Rural Primary Care Recruitment Programs
College of Medicine
State University of New York
Health Science Center at Syracuse
P.O. Box 1000
Binghamton, NY 13902**

I am a high school senior and I am interested in your combined/accelerated medical program (BA/MD). Please send me an application and information concerning your program. Thank you.

**Boston University –
Boston University School of Medicine
Associate Director, Admissions
121 Bay State Road
Boston, MA 02215**

I am a high school senior and I am interested in your combined/accelerated medical program (BA/MD). Please send me an application and information concerning your program. Thank you.

**Brandeis University –
Tufts University School of Medicine
136 Harrison Avenue
Boston, Massachusetts 02111**

I am a high school senior and I am interested in your combined/accelerated medical program (BA/MD). Please send me an application and information concerning your program. Thank you.

NAGENDRA SAI KONERU, M.D.
VINEET ARORA, M.D.
OMAR WANG, ATC

THE HIGH SCHOOL DOCTOR
The Underground Roadmap to 6, 7, and 8 Year
Accelerated/Combined Medical Programs (BA/MD) in the United States

Brooklyn College --
SUNY Health Sciences Center at
Brooklyn
Director of Admissions
Brooklyn College
1602 James Hall
Brooklyn, NY 11210

I am a high school senior and I am interested in your combined/accelerated medical program (BA/MD). Please send me an application and information concerning your program. Thank you.

Brown University –
Brown University School of Medicine
Program in Liberal Medical
Education Office
Box G - A134
Providence, RI 02912

I am a high school senior and I am interested in your combined/accelerated medical program (BA/MD). Please send me an application and information concerning your program. Thank you.

Case Western Reserve University --
Case Western Reserve University
School of Medicine
Office of Undergraduate Admission
10900 Euclid Avenue
Cleveland, OH 44106-7055

I am a high school senior and I am interested in your combined/accelerated medical program (BA/MD). Please send me an application and information concerning your program. Thank you.

NAGENDRA SAI KONERU, M.D.
VINEET ARORA, M.D.
OMAR WANG, ATC

THE HIGH SCHOOL DOCTOR
*The Underground Roadmap to 6, 7, and 8 Year
Accelerated/Combined Medical Programs (BA/MD) in the United States*

**The College of New Jersey -
UMDNJ - New Jersey Medical School
Office of Admissions
New Jersey Medical School
C-653 MSB
185 South Orange Avenue
Newark, NJ 07103-2714**

I am a high school senior and I am interested in your combined/accelerated medical program (BA/MD). Please send me an application and information concerning your program. Thank you.

**The College of William and Mary --
Eastern Virginia Medical School
Office of Admissions
Eastern Virginia Medical School
721 Fairfax Avenue
Norfolk, VA 23507-2000**

I am a high school senior and I am interested in your combined/accelerated medical program (BA/MD). Please send me an application and information concerning your program. Thank you.

**Drew University
UMDNJ - New Jersey Medical School
(MD)
Office of Admissions
New Jersey Medical School
C-653 MSB
185 South Orange Avenue
Newark, NJ 07103-2714**

I am a high school senior and I am interested in your combined/accelerated medical program (BA/MD). Please send me an application and information concerning your program. Thank you.

NAGENDRA SAI KONERU, M.D.
VINEET ARORA, M.D.
OMAR WANG, ATC

THE HIGH SCHOOL DOCTOR
*The Underground Roadmap to 6, 7, and 8 Year
Accelerated/Combined Medical Programs (BA/MD) in the United States*

**Drexel University --
MCP Hahnemann University School
of Medicine
Office of Admissions
3141 Chestnut St.
Philadelphia, PA 19104**

I am a high school senior and I am interested in your combined/accelerated medical program (BA/MD). Please send me an application and information concerning your program. Thank you.

**East Tennessee State University –
East Tennessee State University
School of Medicine
Director, Premedical - Medical
Program
Office of Medical Professions
Advisement
P.O. Box 70,592
Johnson City, TN 37614-0592**

I am a high school senior and I am interested in your combined/accelerated medical program (BA/MD). Please send me an application and information concerning your program. Thank you.

**Fisk University –
Meharry Medical College
Associate Vice President for College
Relations and Lifelong Learning
1005 D.B. Todd, Jr. Boulevard
Nashville, TN 37208**

I am a high school senior and I am interested in your combined/accelerated medical program (BA/MD). Please send me an application and information concerning your program. Thank you.

NAGENDRA SAI KONERU, M.D.
VINEET ARORA, M.D.
OMAR WANG, ATC

THE HIGH SCHOOL DOCTOR
The Underground Roadmap to 6, 7, and 8 Year
Accelerated/Combined Medical Programs (BA/MD) in the United States

George Washington University –
George Washington University
School of Medicine
Office of Admissions
George Washington University
2121 "I" Street, N.W.
Washington, DC 20052

I am a high school senior and I am interested in your combined/accelerated medical program (BA/MD). Please send me an application and information concerning your program. Thank you.

Hampton University --
Eastern Virginia Medical School
Office of Admissions
Eastern Virginia Medical School
721 Fairfax Avenue
Norfolk, VA 23507-2000

I am a high school senior and I am interested in your combined/accelerated medical program (BA/MD). Please send me an application and information concerning your program. Thank you.

Howard University –
Howard University School of Medicine
Center for Preprofessional Education
P.O. Box 473
Administration Building
Washington, DC 20059

I am a high school senior and I am interested in your combined/accelerated medical program (BA/MD). Please send me an application and information concerning your program. Thank you..

NAGENDRA SAI KONERU, M.D.
VINEET ARORA, M.D.
OMAR WANG, ATC

THE HIGH SCHOOL DOCTOR
*The Underground Roadmap to 6, 7, and 8 Year
Accelerated/Combined Medical Programs (BA/MD) in the United States*

**Illinois Institute of Technology --
Chicago Medical School
Director of Admissions
B.S./M.D. Program
Illinois Institute of Technology
10 West 33rd Street
Chicago, IL 60616**

I am a high school senior and I am interested in your combined/accelerated medical program (BA/MD). Please send me an application and information concerning your program. Thank you.

**Kent State University --
Northeastern Ohio Universities
College of Medicine
4209 State Route 44
P.O. Box 95
Rootstown, Ohio 44272**

I am a high school senior and I am interested in your combined/accelerated medical program (BA/MD). Please send me an application and information concerning your program. Thank you.

**Lehigh University --
MCP/Hanneman School of Medicine
Office of Admissions
Lehigh University
27 Memorial Drive West
Bethlehem, PA 18105**

I am a high school senior and I am interested in your combined/accelerated medical program (BA/MD). Please send me an application and information concerning your program. Thank you.

NAGENDRA SAI KONERU, M.D.
VINEET ARORA, M.D.
OMAR WANG, ATC

THE HIGH SCHOOL DOCTOR
The Underground Roadmap to 6, 7, and 8 Year
Accelerated/Combined Medical Programs (BA/MD) in the United States

Michigan State University-
Michigan State University School of Medicine
College of Human Medicine
Office of Admissions
A-239 Life Sciences
East Lansing, MI 48824

I am a high school senior and I am interested in your combined/accelerated medical program (BA/MD). Please send me an application and information concerning your program. Thank you.

Montclair State University --
UMDNJ - New Jersey Medical School
Office of Admissions
New Jersey Medical School
C-653 MSB
185 South Orange Avenue
Newark, NJ 07103-2714

I am a high school senior and I am interested in your combined/accelerated medical program (BA/MD). Please send me an application and information concerning your program. Thank you.

New Jersey Institute of Technology -
UMDNJ - New Jersey Medical School
Office of Admissions
New Jersey Medical School
C-653 MSB
185 South Orange Avenue
Newark, NJ 07103-2714

I am a high school senior and I am interested in your combined/accelerated medical program (BA/MD). Please send me an application and information concerning your program. Thank you.

NAGENDRA SAI KONERU, M.D.
VINEET ARORA, M.D.
OMAR WANG, ATC

THE HIGH SCHOOL DOCTOR
*The Underground Roadmap to 6, 7, and 8 Year
Accelerated/Combined Medical Programs (BA/MD) in the United States*

**New York University –
New York University School of
Medicine
Admissions Office
College of Arts & Science
22 Washington Square North
Room 904 Main Building
New York, NY 10003**

I am a high school senior and I am interested in your combined/accelerated medical program (BA/MD). Please send me an application and information concerning your program. Thank you.

**Norfolk State University --
Eastern Virginia Medical School
Office of Admissions
Eastern Virginia Medical School
721 Fairfax Avenue
Norfolk, VA 23507-2000**

I am a high school senior and I am interested in your combined/accelerated medical program (BA/MD). Please send me an application and information concerning your program. Thank you.

**Northwestern University –
Northwestern University School of
Medicine
Office of Admission and Financial
Aid
1801 Hinman Avenue
Evanston, IL 60204-3060**

I am a high school senior and I am interested in your combined/accelerated medical program (BA/MD). Please send me an application and information concerning your program. Thank you.

NAGENDRA SAI KONERU, M.D.
VINEET ARORA, M.D.
OMAR WANG, ATC

THE HIGH SCHOOL DOCTOR
The Underground Roadmap to 6, 7, and 8 Year
Accelerated/Combined Medical Programs (BA/MD) in the United States

Old Dominion University --
Eastern Virginia Medical School
Office of Admissions
Eastern Virginia Medical School
721 Fairfax Avenue
Norfolk, VA 23507-2000

I am a high school senior and I am interested in your combined/accelerated medical program (BA/MD). Please send me an application and information concerning your program. Thank you.

Pennsylvania State University --
Thomas Jefferson Medical College
Undergraduate Admissions
Pennsylvania State University
201 Shields Building - Box 3000
University Park, PA 16802

I am a high school senior and I am interested in your combined/accelerated medical program (BA/MD). Please send me an application and information concerning your program. Thank you.

Rensselaer Polytechnic Institute --
Albany Medical College
47 New Scotland Avenue
Albany, New York 12208

I am a high school senior and I am interested in your combined/accelerated medical program (BA/MD). Please send me an application and information concerning your program. Thank you.

NAGENDRA SAI KONERU, M.D.
VINEET ARORA, M.D.
OMAR WANG, ATC

THE HIGH SCHOOL DOCTOR
The Underground Roadmap to 6, 7, and 8 Year
Accelerated/Combined Medical Programs (BA/MD) in the United States

Rice University –
Baylor College of Medicine
Office of Admissions
One Baylor Plaza
Room 106A
Houston, TX 77030

I am a high school senior and I am interested in your combined/accelerated medical program (BA/MD). Please send me an application and information concerning your program. Thank you.

Richard Stockton College of New Jersey -
UMDNJ - New Jersey Medical School
Office of Admissions
New Jersey Medical School
C-653 MSB
185 South Orange Avenue
Newark, NJ 07103-2714

I am a high school senior and I am interested in your combined/accelerated medical program (BA/MD). Please send me an application and information concerning your program. Thank you.

Rutgers University -
UMDNJ - Robert Wood Johnson Medical School
Bachelor/Medical Degree Program
Nelson Biological Laboratory
Rutgers University
P.O. Box 1059
Piscataway, NJ 08855-1059

I am a high school senior and I am interested in your combined/accelerated medical program (BA/MD). Please send me an application and information concerning your program. Thank you.

NAGENDRA SAI KONERU, M.D.
VINEET ARORA, M.D.
OMAR WANG, ATC

THE HIGH SCHOOL DOCTOR
*The Underground Roadmap to 6, 7, and 8 Year
Accelerated/Combined Medical Programs (BA/MD) in the United States*

**St. Louis University –
St. Louis University Health Sciences
Center
Scholars Program in Medicine
1402 South Grand Boulevard
St. Louis, MO 63104**

I am a high school senior and I am interested in your combined/accelerated medical program (BA/MD). Please send me an application and information concerning your program. Thank you.

**Siena College --
Albany Medical College
47 New Scotland Avenue
Albany, New York 12208**

I am a high school senior and I am interested in your combined/accelerated medical program (BA/MD). Please send me an application and information concerning your program. Thank you.

**State University of New York at
Stony Brook –
SUNY Stony Brook Health Sciences
Center
Scholars In Medicine Program
Honors College
Stony Brook, New York 11794-3357**

I am a high school senior and I am interested in your combined/accelerated medical program (BA/MD). Please send me an application and information concerning your program. Thank you.

NAGENDRA SAI KONERU, M.D.
VINEET ARORA, M.D.
OMAR WANG, ATC

THE HIGH SCHOOL DOCTOR
*The Underground Roadmap to 6, 7, and 8 Year
Accelerated/Combined Medical Programs (BA/MD) in the United States*

**Stevens Institute of Technology --
UMDNJ - New Jersey Medical School
(MD)
Office of Admissions
New Jersey Medical School
C-653 MSB
185 South Orange Avenue
Newark, NJ 07103-2714**

I am a high school senior and I am interested in your combined/accelerated medical program (BA/MD). Please send me an application and information concerning your program. Thank you.

**Tufts University --
Tufts University School of Medicine
136 Harrison Avenue
Boston, Massachusetts 02111**

I am a high school senior and I am interested in your combined/accelerated medical program (BA/MD). Please send me an application and information concerning your program. Thank you..

**Union College --
Albany Medical College
47 New Scotland Avenue
Albany, New York 12208**

I am a high school senior and I am interested in your combined/accelerated medical program (BA/MD). Please send me an application and information concerning your program. Thank you.

NAGENDRA SAI KONERU, M.D.
VINEET ARORA, M.D.
OMAR WANG, ATC

THE HIGH SCHOOL DOCTOR
*The Underground Roadmap to 6, 7, and 8 Year
Accelerated/Combined Medical Programs (BA/MD) in the United States*

**University of Akron --
Northeastern Ohio Universities
College of Medicine
4209 State Route 44
P.O. Box 95
Rootstown, Ohio 44272**

I am a high school senior and I am interested in your combined/accelerated medical program (BA/MD). Please send me an application and information concerning your program. Thank you..

**University of Alabama –
University of Alabama School of
Medicine
UAB Office of Enrollment
Management
272 Hill University Center
Birmingham, AL 35294**

I am a high school senior and I am interested in your combined/accelerated medical program (BA/MD). Please send me an application and information concerning your program. Thank you.

**University of California at Riverside –
University of California – Los Angeles
School of Medicine
Biomedical Sciences Program
Los Angeles, California 90095**

I am a high school senior and I am interested in your combined/accelerated medical program (BA/MD). Please send me an application and information concerning your program. Thank you..

NAGENDRA SAI KONERU, M.D.
VINEET ARORA, M.D.
OMAR WANG, ATC

THE HIGH SCHOOL DOCTOR
The Underground Roadmap to 6, 7, and 8 Year
Accelerated/Combined Medical Programs (BA/MD) in the United States

**University of Miami –
University of Miami School of
Medicine
P.O. Box 248025
Coral Gables, FL 33124**

I am a high school senior and I am interested in your combined/accelerated medical program (BA/MD). Please send me an application and information concerning your program. Thank you.

**University of Michigan –
University of Michigan School of
Medicine
Interflex Program
5113 Medical Science I Building,
Wing C
Ann Arbor, MI 48109-0611**

I am a high school senior and I am interested in your combined/accelerated medical program (BA/MD). Please send me an application and information concerning your program. Thank you..

**University of Missouri-Columbia --
University of Missouri-Columbia
School of Medicine
Conley Scholars Program
One Hospital Drive, Columbia,
Missouri 65212
University of Missouri-Columbia**

I am a high school senior and I am interested in your combined/accelerated medical program (BA/MD). Please send me an application and information concerning your program. Thank you.

NAGENDRA SAI KONERU, M.D.
VINEET ARORA, M.D.
OMAR WANG, ATC

THE HIGH SCHOOL DOCTOR
*The Underground Roadmap to 6, 7, and 8 Year
Accelerated/Combined Medical Programs (BA/MD) in the United States*

**University of Missouri Kansas City
School of Medicine
Council on Selection
2411 Holmes
Kansas City, MO 64108**

I am a high school senior and I am interested in your combined/accelerated medical program (BA/MD). Please send me an application and information concerning your program. Thank you.

**University of Rochester –
University of Rochester School of Medicine
Program Coordinator
Rochester Early Medical Scholars
Meliora Hall
Rochester, NY 14627**

I am a high school senior and I am interested in your combined/accelerated medical program (BA/MD). Please send me an application and information concerning your program. Thank you.

**University of South Alabama –
South Alabama School of Medicine
Office of Admissions
Administrative Building, Room 182
Mobile, AL 36688-0002**

I am a high school senior and I am interested in your combined/accelerated medical program (BA/MD). Please send me an application and information concerning your program. Thank you.

NAGENDRA SAI KONERU, M.D.
VINEET ARORA, M.D.
OMAR WANG, ATC

THE HIGH SCHOOL DOCTOR
*The Underground Roadmap to 6, 7, and 8 Year
Accelerated/Combined Medical Programs (BA/MD) in the United States*

**University of Southern California –
University of Southern California
School of Medicine
College of Letters, Arts and Sciences
University of Southern California
CAS 100, University Park
Los Angeles, California 90089-0152**

I am a high school senior and I am interested in your combined/accelerated medical program (BA/MD). Please send me an application and information concerning your program. Thank you.

**University of Wisconsin at Madison –
University of Wisconsin at Madison
Medical School
Medical Scholars Program
1300 University Avenue, Room 1250
Madison, WI 53706**

I am a high school senior and I am interested in your combined/accelerated medical program (BA/MD). Please send me an application and information concerning your program. Thank you.

**Villanova University --
MCP/ Hahnemann School of
Medicine
Office of Undergraduate Admissions
Villanova University
800 Lancaster Avenue
Villanova, PA 19085-1699**

I am a high school senior and I am interested in your combined/accelerated medical program (BA/MD). Please send me an application and information concerning your program. Thank you.

NAGENDRA SAI KONERU, M.D.
VINEET ARORA, M.D.
OMAR WANG, ATC

THE HIGH SCHOOL DOCTOR
*The Underground Roadmap to 6, 7, and 8 Year
Accelerated/Combined Medical Programs (BA/MD) in the United States*

Virginia Commonwealth University
Guaranteed Admissions Programs
Honors Program
Anne L. Chandler, Ph.D.
920 W Franklin Street
PO Box 843010
Richmond, VA 23284-3010

I am a high school senior and I am interested in your combined/accelerated medical program (BA/MD). Please send me an application and information concerning your program. Thank you.

Youngstown University --
Northeastern Ohio Universities
College of Medicine
4209 State Route 44
P.O. Box 95
Rootstown, Ohio 44272

I am a high school senior and I am interested in your combined/accelerated medical program (BA/MD). Please send me an application and information concerning your program. Thank you.

About the Authors

Nagendra Sai Koneru, MD

Although born in Hyderabad, India, Nagendra Sai Koneru moved to Chicago at the age of three. Nagendra is the son of Dr. Nagabhushanam and Srimani Koneru. He remained in the Chicago suburbs throughout his education prior to college. He is known to friends as just "Bobby". He attended Hoffman Estates High School in Illinois where he was active in Newspaper, Math Team, and Tennis. He was awarded the MVP award for the varsity team during his sophomore year for tennis, an award normally given to Seniors. He qualified for the state tournament during his senior year and finished in the top thirty for the state of Illinois. Nagendra was also an active member of the National Honor Society. He volunteered at the local Hospital for four years and taught Hispanics mathematics at the YMCA for two years. He attended the Argonne National Labs Summer Internship For Gifted Students during his Junior year. Nagendra eventually graduated in the top five percent of his class as an Illinois State Scholar and was accepted into the eight year BA/MD program at the University of Missouri-Columbia as a Conley Scholar.

During his career at the University of Missouri-Columbia, Nagendra was active in leadership roles. He was a newspaper reporter for the local paper *The Maneater*. He was also involved in the pursuit of his own spirituality. He created a newsletter and organization entitled *Vedanta* which explored the ideas of Hinduism, Buddhism, and Taoism. Nagendra matriculated into the University of Missouri-Columbia School of Medicine where he founded the first Radiology student interest group. His interest in Radiology grew as he finished his medical school training. Days before his graduation, he was joined in marriage to Sarita Koneru. He compiled and wrote the major bulk of *The High School Doctor* which he started with Vineet Arora five years prior. Nagendra has also authored a book entitled *The Best Foreign Medical Schools: The Underground Roadmap from Foreign Medical School to U.S. Residency*. He is currently doing a year of Research in Radiology and plans to pursue a career as a Radiologist.

Vineet Arora, MD

Originally from Rockville, Maryland, Vineet Arora remained relatively local in during her undergraduate years in Baltimore, at the Johns Hopkins University. Here, in addition to her premedical studies, she tutored economics and sociology, spent many nights working for the Office of Alumni Affairs as a telephone fundraiser, and was the student organizer for the Welch Lecture Series in Medical topics. She completed her undergraduate education in three years, graduated Phi Beta Kappa in 1994, and relocated to the Midwest for medical school. During her career at Washington University in St. Louis, she cofounded and served as the editor for the student newspaper *Auscultations*, chaired the faculty nobel laureate social society to improve faculty student interaction, and taught local elementary school students about the perils of drug and alcohol abuse. During a panel for Washington University undergraduates interested in medicine, she addressed many questions facing medical school applicants, and life in medicine. It was after this panel that she started to compile the initial research and write the first chapters of the High School Doctor. During residency, she continued her interest in advising premedical students at the University of Chicago via panel discussions for undergraduates. She recently completed her internal medicine at the University of Chicago and will be serving as the chief medical resident for the University of Chicago in 2002. Currently, she is jointly completing a general medicine fellowship and a Masters in Public Policy with a concentration in healthcare policy. In her spare time, she enjoys running, catching up with friends, and backpacking off the beaten path through her favorite foreign countries.

Omar Wang, ATC

For the past seven years as an athletic trainer, Omar has had the opportunity to work with a number of physicians who specializes in Orthopedics and Internal Medicine. Currently, Omar is in his second year working as an Assistant Athletic Trainer for Mercer University located in Macon, Georgia. He is also currently working on his second Master's Degree in Business Administration. Before coming to Mercer University, he was at Florida Atlantic University in Boca Raton, Florida working as the Men's Basketball Athletic Trainer. Prior to arriving at Florida Atlantic University, Omar obtained his first Master's Degree in Athletic Training at West Virginia University in Morgantown, West Virginia University in May 1999. While at West Virginia University, he worked as the Baseball and Wrestling Graduate Assistant Athletic Trainer. In May 1996, he received his Bachelor's Degree in Movement Science at the University of Michigan in Ann Arbor. For two years at the University of Michigan, he worked as a student athletic trainer. After he graduated from the University of Michigan, he worked as an Assistant Athletic Trainer at Neosho County Community College in Chanute, Kansas. Omar is a native of South Barrington, Illinois. He is a member of the National Athletic Trainers' Association, American Red Cross, and the Georgia Athletic Trainers' Association. He is also a certified strength and conditioning specialist and a personal trainer by the National Strength and Conditioning Association.

Printed in the United States
24920LVS00001B/37